WHITEFIELD & WESLEY
ON THE NEW BIRTH

WHITEFIELD & WESLEY ON THE NEW BIRTH

Timothy L. Smith

FRANCIS ASBURY PRESS
of Zondervan Publishing House

Grand Rapids, Michigan

WHITEFIELD AND WESLEY ON THE NEW BIRTH

Copyright © 1986 by Timothy L. Smith

FRANCIS ASBURY PRESS
is an imprint of Zondervan Publishing House
1415 Lake Drive S.E., Grand Rapids, Michigan 49506

Library of Congress Cataloging in Publication Data

Whitefield, George, 1714–1770.
  Whitefield & Wesley on the New Birth.

  Regeneration (Theology)—Early works to 1800. 2. Conversion—Early works to
1800. I. Wesley, John, 1703–1791. II. Smith, Timothy Lawrence, 1924–
III. Title. IV. Title: Whitefield and Wesley on the New Birth.
BT790.W48   1986   234'.4   86–15878
ISBN 0-310-75151-9

Designed by Louise M. Bauer
Edited by Anne P. Root

Printed in the United States of America

86 87 88 89 90 91 92 93 94 95 / 10 9 8 7 6 5 4 3 2 1

TO
LARRY

Contents

Preface

Aside from Luke Tyerman, a nineteenth-century Methodist, few historians have read and pondered the writings of both George Whitefield and John Wesley. Most have belonged, as Tyerman did, to one or the other partisan camp and allowed their knowledge of that tradition to guide their judgments. Preoccupation with supposed preeminence or priority has distorted their view of the two men's early cooperation.

Whitefield was, of course, Wesley's protégé and great admirer during his Oxford years. On the other hand, Whitefield was the first one of the Oxford group to emerge into eminence as a preacher, doing so while John Wesley was still unknown to most Englishmen and caught in the morass of his mission to Georgia. Whitefield also became a missionary to Georgia, but he became established as a notable preacher in England before he left, while Wesley was still overseas. On his return late in 1738 Whitefield began preaching in the open air and became the leader of an extensive revival in the west port of Bristol. In late March, 1739, he persuaded Wesley to take his place so he could return to America. From that point forward, the less well-known Wesley slowly achieved eminence on his own. But he never lost his admiration for Whitefield as a preacher, and Whitefield never lost his tendency to defer to Wesley as scholar, theologian and spiritual guide.

Most important, although they fell into controversy during 1740 over predestination and Wesley's teaching about heart purity, they continued to act together for the spiritual renewal of the Church of England, in which they were both clergymen. Though one became an Arminian perfectionist while the other withdrew somewhat from the perfectionistic view of regeneration he had earlier expressed, neither Wesley nor the increasingly Calvinist Whitefield ever altered his basic stance on the primacy of the experience of the new birth. For this reason, and because these two preachers together were largely responsible for setting the course that popular evangelicalism has followed to the present time, I thought it would be profitable for both scholarly and religious readers to study their careers side by side and read their testimonies and sermons together.

In republishing their writings I have relied, with two exceptions, on

7

the earliest English editions. In later ones, both men followed the eighteenth-century custom of freely amending their writings, and both men tended in editing to clarify or eliminate material which beclouded understanding of their theological positions. Whitefield wrote few theological tracts. However, this book includes key portions of one by Wesley, along with an open letter and a selection from the minutes of the first Methodist conference. I wish to show the two great evangelists at the height of their agreement over the nature of the experience of regeneration, without making Whitefield seem an Arminian or Wesley a Calvinist.

The accounts each man wrote of his conversion experience and the texts of their sermons, including one that Whitefield wrote and Wesley edited and published for him in June, 1739, are useful both as historical benchmarks and as present-day religious inspiration. The doctrine of new birth in Christ has never, I think, been more eloquently and clearly set forth than by these two men. John Wesley, who was eleven years older, was to hold center stage in the history of English evangelicalism for forty-five years; Whitefield, while remaining very influential in England, enjoyed a similar position in America until his death in 1769.

Though relying on original editions of their writings, I have changed the spelling to conform to modern practice—for example, dropping the English "u" from words such as "honour" and "Saviour" and writing "gaol" as "jail." I have changed the familiar "ye," "thee," "thou," and "thine" to "you" or "your" and modernized present-tense verbs, even in quotations from Scripture (though not in poetry, hymns, or anthems), and pruned away dashes and capitalizations of ordinary nouns. Occasionally I have added in brackets an "and" or a "so," or some such word, to make the sense clear; but if these were substituted for another word or phrase, I have indicated it with an ellipsis of three dots. Longer ellipses of four dots represent a section left out because it seemed less relevant or necessary. I have also altered the punctuation, freely substituting periods for semicolons and commas for exclamation points where doing so did not seem to disturb the meaning of the passage. And I have corrected a very few obvious mistakes in verb tenses or grammar, assuming that some of these were misprints.

I wish to express my very great thanks to Frank Baker, professor of theology at Duke University and editor of the now combined Oxford and Bicentennial Editions of Wesley's works. A giant among Methodist scholars, he has guided me to Wesley's original texts, and encouraged me to do my own editing of all that appears in this little book. The librarians at Oxford and Cambridge universities, at the British Library and the Dr. Williams Library in London, at Vanderbilt and Boston universities, and at the Boston Athenaeum and Boston Public libraries have responded to many requests, as have those at my own Johns Hopkins University. Darryl Hart, a doctoral candidate at Hopkins, has worked with the texts, aiding Debi Belt, who carefully typed the entire manuscript.

The greatest inspiration for this book, however, came from my many evangelical friends in England and America, especially those teaching and studying at earnestly Christian institutions. I saw in them, and hundreds of others like them, persons who needed to know how close Calvinists and Arminians—and indeed evangelicals of Lutheran, Anglican, and Peace-Church persuasions as well—have always been in their teaching about regeneration.

ALL SAINTS DAY, 1985
Timothy L. Smith

INTRODUCTION:
GEORGE WHITEFIELD AND
THE WESLEYAN WITNESS*

by Timothy L. Smith

Three religious impulses lay behind the evangelical movement that emerged in England during the 1730s, when John and Charles Wesley drew together at Oxford University the company of students scornfully labeled "Methodists." One was the Anglican moralism that started John Wesley on his spiritual pilgrimage. Inspired by his parents, particularly his mother Susanna, Wesley soon concluded that the call to righteousness pervading the Old and the New Testaments was the central theme of Scripture. He read such works as Jeremy Taylor's *Holy Living and Holy Dying* and William Law's *Serious Call to a Devout and Holy Life*. And he set out in earnest to find by God's grace that "holiness, without which no man shall see the Lord."[1]

The second impulse was the persisting force of Calvinistic elements within Puritanism, a movement that had turned England first to prayer and then to political revolution in the preceding century. The Puritan movement subsided with the restoration of the Stuart monarchy in 1660, and the crowning of William and Mary thirty-eight years later reinforced the growing aversion to all forms of intense piety. Puritan fervor and moral seriousness persisted, not only in Anglican parishes (all four of Wesley's grandparents were Puritans) but in Presbyterian Scotland and among the dissenting Baptists, Presbyterians, and Congregationalists of England and America. Meanwhile, on both sides of the Atlantic, George Fox's Society of Friends propagated their radical commitment to moral discipline and their belief that the light of Christ, usually identified with the Holy Spirit, awakened the conscience, or "seed," that remained alive in fallen human hearts.[2]

---

*The original version of this introduction appeared in *The Wesleyan Theological Journal* 19 (Spring 1984): 63–85.

The third impulse stemmed from German Pietism. This movement of prayer, Bible study, and corporate discipline brought laypersons and pastors into hundreds of local associations intent on renewing the spiritual life of the established Lutheran or Calvinist churches. By the time the Wesleys were completing their studies at Oxford, the Pietists had established an orphan house and training school at what later became the University of Halle in Saxony, and had begun sending missionaries to the cities of the Old World and the frontiers of the New. In 1722, Count Nicholas Ludwig von Zinzendorf, a Pietist, allowed an intensely spiritual group of Moravians, from what is now Czechoslovakia, to settle at Herrnhut, on his new estate in Saxony. Within a few years, the growing settlement launched the missionary movement that became the Moravian Church.[3]

In the summer of 1734 George Whitefield, nineteen years old and a poor widow's son, entered Pembroke College in Oxford, earning his keep as a servant waiting on better-off students. Shy and self-conscious, he was already in deep search of saving faith. Charles Wesley befriended him and gave him Pietist August Hermann Francke's tract *Against the Fear of Man* and, a bit later, Henry Scougal's *Life of God in the Soul of Man*. During the following months with the Wesleys, as Whitefield wrote in 1739, "religion began to take root in my heart, and I was fully convinced my soul must be totally renewed ere it could see God." Whitefield's recently published letters make clear that as early as 1735 the idea of the new birth, though not the instantaneous assurance of it, was a commonplace among the Oxford Methodists. Two years later, Whitefield was ordained a deacon in the Church of England and began preaching on the new birth with notable success in his native city of Gloucester as well as at London, Bristol, and other places. In 1737, following in the steps of the two Wesleys, he sought and received appointment to go to Georgia as chaplain to the new colony being established there.[4]

Before his departure, Whitefield's sermon *On the Nature and Necessity of Our Regeneration or New Birth in Christ Jesus*, based on the text "if any man be in Christ he is a new creature" (2 Cor. 5:17), appeared in London, the first of many English and American editions.[5] It is reprinted below. John Wesley, still in Georgia, did not yet enjoy the experience Whitefield's sermon described, and returned to England the following winter conscious of his great need of it.[6] Wesley's earlier sermons, however, especially two that he preached at Oxford in 1733—"The Circumcision of the Heart" and a borrowed one, "Grieve Not the Holy Spirit of God"—and several others that were until recently attributed to Charles Wesley, show that before their earliest contacts with Moravian teachers, the Holy Club was moving in close accord toward the doctrines that were to become central in the evangelical awakenings.[7]

Of these, Whitefield declared in the sermon of 1737, "the doctrine of our regeneration, or new birth in Christ Jesus" is "one of the most fundamental." It is a "fatal mistake," he warned, to "put asunder what God has inseparably joined together" and to "expect to be justified by Christ" without also being sanctified, that is, having one's nature "changed and made holy." Many, he continued, "are baptized with water, which were never, effectually at least, baptized with the Holy Ghost." To be "born again" implies "an inward change and purity of heart, and cohabitation of his Holy Spirit." It means "to be mystically united to Him by a true and lively faith, and thereby to receive spiritual virtue from Him, as. . .branches from the vine." To be thus "made anew" is necessary to our happiness in heaven. Hence the "irrevocable decree of the Almighty, that *without holiness*, that is, without being made pure by regeneration, and having the image of God thereby reinstamped upon the soul, *no man living shall see the Lord.*" In his closing appeal, Whitefield asked, "Have we receiv'd the Holy Ghost since we believed? Are we *new creatures* in Christ or no?" Nothing but "the wedding garment of *a new nature*" will suffice. "Unless the Spirit, which raised Jesus from the dead, dwell in you here," he concluded, "neither will your mortal bodies be quickened by the same Spirit to dwell with Him hereafter."[8]

The doctrines of this discourse, though not all its pentecostal proof texts, parallel those of John Wesley's sermon on "Salvation by Faith," also reprinted below. Wesley wrote and preached it before Oxford University in June, 1738, two weeks after his experience of "living faith" at a prayer meeting in Aldersgate Street, London.[9] Both sermons proclaimed to all the world the three points of Christian belief upon which Whitefield, soon to become a full-fledged Calvinist, and John and Charles Wesley, who opposed the Calvinistic system, always agreed. Indeed, they shared these convictions with Quakers and Baptists, with the German Pietists, Mennonites, and Moravians, and with a growing majority of the heirs of the Puritans, whether Presbyterian, Anglican, or Congregationalist, in Great Britain and America. All such "evangelicals" affirmed the moral authority of the Bible, declaring that it called human beings to a righteousness that is not only imputed to them in Christ's name but actually imparted to them by His grace. All stressed the work of the Holy Spirit in bringing sinners to repentance and faith in Christ, assuring them of forgiveness, and, by His presence thereafter in their hearts, nurturing in them the love and holiness that please God. Evangelicals also declared it the duty of all who had discovered these truths and experienced this grace to proclaim the good news of salvation everywhere, at home and abroad.[10] From that day until this, these three convictions have marked the boundaries of evangelical Protestantism.

The Bible is its authority, the new birth its hallmark, and evangelism its mission.[11]

Whitefield returned from Georgia for his ordination to the Anglican priesthood in November, 1738. In London, Bristol, and several towns between them, the revivals that had begun under his earlier preaching broke out afresh. The transformed evangelism of the Wesleys had given a new impulse to the revivals, as had that of the Moravian missionaries, particularly in London.[12] Whitefield's American experience had accustomed him to preaching in dissenting houses of worship and, occasionally, in the open air. Now, whether excluded or not from Anglican pulpits, he greatly expanded both practices.[13] Campaigning through Wales in March, while the great revival at the nearby port of Bristol was getting underway, he met and formed an alliance with young Howell Harris, some of whose Welsh societies afterwards became the nucleus of the Calvinistic Methodist Church.[14] During those same months, however, John Wesley was earnestly seeking a fuller "witness of the Spirit" to the new life in Christ he had found at Aldersgate. I have "peace with God," he wrote shortly afterwards, "and I sin not today." But the joy he thought Scripture promised eluded him.[15]

Whitefield's *Journals* and published letters show how fully he agreed with the Wesleys that "nothing but an assurance that we are born again, that we are members of CHRIST, that we are united to Him by one and the same Spirit with which He himself was actuated" can "satisfy the heart of man."[16] The three men also agreed on the nature and extent of the sanctification begun through the work of the Holy Spirit in regeneration.[17] Whitefield preached often and printed repeatedly, his second published sermon, "The Marks of the New Birth," which he later issued under the title, "Marks of Having Received the Holy Ghost."[18] In it, he linked the question St. Paul asked the Ephesian believers—"Have you received the Holy Ghost since you believed?" (Acts 19:2)—to the experience of the apostles at Pentecost. The miracles that accompanied their experience are not necessary, Whitefield declared, "but it is absolutely necessary that we should receive the Holy Ghost in his sanctifying graces as really as they did, and so will it continue to be till the end of the world." We must "be baptized with his baptism and refining fire, before we can be styled true members" of Christ's "mystical body." That experience accomplishes the aim of Christ's coming, namely, to make those who believe on Him "partakers of the divine nature" and restore them to "that primitive dignity" in which they were "at first created." Christ's atonement, Whitefield continued, "purchased again for us the Holy Ghost," so that He might "once more reinstamp the divine image upon our hearts, and make us capable of living with and enjoying

God."[19] One who was thus born of the Spirit would "not willfully commit sin, much less live in the habitual practice of it." Rather, on any fall into evil such a true believer quickly repents, and afterwards "takes double heed to his ways . . . and perfects holiness in the fear of God."[20] Here, in short, was a view of regeneration that in substance matched precisely what the two Wesleys had been preaching for nearly twelve months, and for which they found the doors of Anglican churches closed against them.[21]

Little wonder that as the time drew near for Whitefield to return to Georgia, he urged John Wesley to come to Bristol and assume the leadership of the revival there. Wesley arrived the first of April, 1739, and undertook the open-air preaching he had hitherto loathed.[22] Speaking several times each day, he began systematic expositions of the doctrines of the evangelical awakening in concurrent series of sermons on the Gospel of John, the Sermon on the Mount, the opening chapters of the Acts of the Apostles, and Paul's Epistle to the Romans.[23] Meanwhile, Whitefield's departure was delayed for some months by the French embargo. This enabled him not only to spread the revival to other towns, but to join the Wesleys frequently in public and private meetings at Bristol and London.[24]

The unity of the three men was everywhere apparent during this crucial summer; and they muted the single point of disagreement among them, the doctrine of predestination. John Wesley set forth his long standing objections to that doctrine in a sermon entitled "Free Grace," written and preached at Bristol in late April; but in response to Whitefield's pleas, he did not preach it again and deferred publishing it for many months.[25] They and their helpers affirmed, from a broad range of scriptural texts, what Whitefield called "the reasonableness of the doctrine of the new birth, and the necessity of our receiving the Holy Ghost in his sanctifying gifts and graces" in connection with it. They scorned the charge that expecting the Holy Spirit to deliver seekers from the power as well as the guilt of willful sin was "enthusiasm."[26] All three taught that concrete acts of charity to suffering human beings—orphans, poor families, persons in prison, and victims of war or national disasters—must blossom in the midst of any authentic spiritual awakening. Whitefield was no less than the Wesleys the advocate of a socially concerned Christianity. And he grounded that concern as earnestly as they did in the law of Moses and Jesus that God's people must love their neighbors as themselves.[27] All three resisted heartily the Moravian notion of "stillness," namely, that seekers must not exercise any effort, either by prayer, repentance, or good works, nor share in Holy Communion until, in Whitefield's words, they had "received the Holy

Ghost in the full assurance of it" as the apostles did at Pentecost.[28] And they rejected those called "French prophets," several of whom were women, for insisting that "extraordinary gifts of the Spirit (such as the trances, exorcism, speaking in unknown languages, and miracles of healing recorded in the church of Pentecost) should accompany what Whitefield and the Wesleys always called His "ordinary gifts," namely, "righteousness, peace, and joy in the Holy Ghost."[29]

The doctrine of the sanctifying Spirit thus became as crucial to the evangelical awakening, as it had been, in Geoffrey Nuttall's accounting, to the Puritan movement of the preceding century. During a week of evangelism with John Wesley in Bristol and nearby Bath in July, Whitefield wrote and Wesley helped edit for immediate publication his sermon *On the Indwelling Spirit, the Common Privilege of All Believers*, from the text in John 7:37–39, which appears below. It was reprinted many times in the next few years and, with only minor editing, included in Whitefield's collection of his revised discourses, published in 1745.[30] The theme of the sermon, like that of the one on "The Marks of the New Birth," was the promise of Jesus that His followers should receive the Holy Spirit, not so that they might work miracles or show "outward signs and wonders" but in order to be partakers of "His sanctifying graces."[31] The fact of original sin, in Whitefield's view, made this promise reasonable. "The great work of sanctification, or making us holy," he said, belonged to "the sanctifying Spirit promised in the text"; He would restore those who "truly believe" to the "glorious liberties of the sons of God."[32] Before his departure for America in mid-August, Whitefield also wrote and published *The Power of Christ's Resurrection*, based on Philippians 3:10, which reiterated these points. Its central question was, as Whitefield put it, whether or not believers "have received the Holy Ghost, and by his powerful operation in our hearts been raised from the death of sin to a life of righteousness and true holiness."[33] During the year that followed he made that question the key to a broad extension of the religious awakenings then going on in the towns of New England and the Middle Colonies.[34]

Meanwhile, growing disagreement with the Moravians moved the Wesleys steadily toward the conviction that some of the biblical passages they and Whitefield had been using to describe the new birth referred primarily to a second and deeper experience of hallowing grace.[35] John Wesley's renewed study and repeated exposition during the late summer and fall of 1739 of the opening sentences of Jesus' Sermon on the Mount (which likely yielded the essence of the three discourses he published on those sentences seven years later) may have catalyzed that conviction.[36] From that time on he taught that to be made "pure in heart" and filled with love for God and man was the essence of Christian perfection, and that this "second benefit" was promised to those who, in poverty of spirit, meekness, and mourning, were already born into the family of God and made heirs of His kingdom.[37] On November 7 and 8, after a crucial encounter with the Moravian Bishop August G. Spangenberg, John Wesley may have composed some of his widely read condensation of the early chapter of William Law's *Christian Perfection*, published the next year. Either then or during the next few days he probably composed the momentous sermon entitled "Christian Perfection" that he published in September, 1741; for on November 12 and again on Saturday evening, November 17, he explained to small gatherings of his followers "the nature and extent of Christian perfection," words that point to the sermon's contents.[38]

During the following winter Wesley preached important sermons from a group of texts he always thereafter used to declare the promise of full cleansing from the corruption of "inbred sin" that remains in believers after they are born again. Among those texts were 2 Peter 1:4; 1 John 1:7 and 2:12; Ephesians 4:23–24; and Hebrews 4:9 and 10:19.[39] In the spring of 1740 he published a scriptural account of the two moments of grace by which he had come to believe the Spirit made sinners whole—characteristically, in the preface to a hymnbook, the second volume of *Hymns and Sacred Poems*,[40] on which he and his brother collaborated. That preface, reprinted with only slight revision twenty-six years later in his *Plain Account of Christian Perfection*, remained for the rest of John Wesley's life the benchmark of his doctrine of inward holiness.[41]

During these months, however, Whitefield's theological sensibilities were subject to quite different influences. Whether he left England unaware that his friends were moving rapidly toward the idea of a second and "entirely" sanctifying moment of grace is unclear. In a letter to a Scottish minister written in early August, 1739, the young evangelist rejoiced that the revival spirit had spread to that country. Then he added, in response to a complaint that seems almost too early to have been aimed at the Wesleys, "I follow them as they follow CHRIST. I am no friend of sinless perfection. I believe the being (though not the dominion) of sin remains in the hearts of the greatest believers." (His "greatest believers," of course, were John Wesley's "young men in Christ"—persons who had received the "abiding witness of the Spirit" to their new birth.)[42] The sermon Whitefield enclosed with this letter may have been another he wrote and published that summer under the title *A Preservative Against Unsettled Notions, and Want of Principles, in regard to Righteousness and Christian Perfection*. Its text, Ecclesiastes 7:16, "Be not righteous overmuch," had been used to attack the Methodists.

Whitefield's sermon explained that the biblical writer's actual purpose was "to exhort the *truly righteous*" to continue in "constant pursuit of greater and greater *perfection* and *righteousness*, till they rest in Christ." He declared that Yahweh's appeal to Abraham, "Walk thou before me, and be thou perfect," as well as the passage in Deuteronomy 18:13, "You shall be blameless before the Lord thy God," were the basis of Jesus' exhortation in Matthew 5:48, "Be ye therefore perfect, even as your Father which is in heaven is perfect."[43]

Other evidence of Whitefield's uncertainty appears in his *Journals.* During his first days aboard ship, he plunged into writing the *Short Account* of his early life that he sent back for John Wesley to publish. It radiated the language of the Methodist awakening, emphasizing the work of the Holy Spirit both in regeneration and in bringing believers up to "the measure of His fulness who filleth all in all."[44] But his journal for the remainder of the voyage to Philadelphia revealed a growing struggle. "I was frequently enlightened to see the pride and selfishness of my heart," he stated on August 25, "and as frequently longed for that perfect liberty wherewith Christ sets his servants free." Two weeks later he wrote, "I groan daily to be set at liberty. Dearest Redeemer, I come unto Thee weary and heavy laden. Oh, do Thou bring me into the full freedom of the sons of God." The shame of his past sins often oppressed him.[45]

During the latter part of the voyage, Whitefield read and found himself approving the writings of certain "Cambridge Puritans," who championed imputed righteousness and charged that Arminians relied upon their own works for justification. When a Quaker on board preached reliance upon "Christ *within* and not Christ *without*, as the fountain of our faith," Whitefield commented that "the outward righteousness of Jesus Christ imputed to us" is "the sole fountain and cause" of all that believers receive from the Spirit of God.[46] On October 13 he expressed gratitude for the "blessed teachings of His Holy Spirit" during the previous weeks. They had convinced him, he said, "of the pride, sensuality, and blindness" of his heart.[47]

On his arrival at Philadelphia November 3, the young evangelist found his way prepared by the news of the awakenings in England. Encouraging him on was the spirituality of the Quakers and of the "fifteen denominations of German Christians" that flourished in the area, and the growing influence of the Presbyterian pastor-revivalists William and Gilbert Tennant, founders of the "log college" from whence Princeton sprang. Within a few weeks, Whitefield breathed new life into their efforts and brought thousands of people in towns from Wilmington, Delaware, to New York City face to face with the evangelical call to be born again.[48]

At the end of the month Whitefield composed his great sermon,

"The Lord our Righteousness." Its major purpose was to declare, from the messianic text in Jeremiah 23:5–6, that Christ dealt with human sinfulness by imputing to believers His perfect righteousness.[49] The sermon was not a digression from Methodist doctrine, but an exposition of one major facet of it, as a comparison with John Wesley's later sermon on the same text and his many summaries of the same point will show.[50] Whitefield acknowledged "the unChristian walk" of some who "talked of Christ's imputed righteousness." But he insisted, as Wesley often did, that the teaching of Jesus and Paul only excluded good works "from being any cause of our justification in the sight of God." Doing them, Whitefield declared, was "a proof of our having this righteousness imputed to us"; and he warned that "an unapplied Christ is no Christ at all." For the text, he said, promised not only "Christ's personal righteousness imputed to us, but also holiness of heart wrought in us. These two God has joined together. He never did, He never does, He never will put them asunder. If you are justified by the *Blood*, you are also sanctified by the Spirit of our Lord." [51] All this from a young Anglican priest not yet twenty-four years of age, whose spiritual pilgrimage had begun only five years before!

Clearly, however, during the very months when John Wesley thought he discovered that the promise of heart purity pervaded both the Old and New Testaments and staked the future of his movement upon it, Whitefield, reveling in America's awakening, allowed sanctification to become a secondary concern. His journal and correspondence written during this second American journey (November 1739 to December 1740), while he preached his way from Pennsylvania to Georgia twice and then from Georgia to Boston and back again, indicate a growing alignment of his beliefs and sensibilities with those of the Calvinist pastors in the colonies—Presbyterians, Congregationalists, and Baptists. None of these were friends of either free grace or Christian perfection.[52] Hints also recur that although the young clergyman realized that his personal quest of holiness was being frustrated, the immense response to his preaching made the frustration less painful.[53]

Because several bundles of letters sent across the Atlantic were misdirected and only slowly forwarded, Whitefield spent this year of evangelism in America largely out of touch with his English friends. He did not learn for many months that soon after his departure John Wesley decided to publish his sermon on "Free Grace" and began clearly to proclaim and set his closest followers to seeking the experience of heart purity and perfect love. He received a letter from Wesley in March that has not survived. But it prompted him to write pleading that they quarrel no more, either over the doctrine of predestination (of which, Whitefield declared, he was "ten thousand times more convinced" than when he left England) or over Wesley's belief that certain Scriptures promised full deliverance from the "strugglings of indwelling sin." Two months later, Whitefield warned in another letter that he also differed from Wesley's "notions about committing sin." Since the American revivals were being carried on without divisions over these issues, he hoped Wesley had no plans to come there and thought it might be best that he not return to England.[54]

A few hours after Whitefield arrived in Boston on September 20, 1740, he wrote in his journal that though refreshed by accounts of the success of the gospel in "several packets of letters . . . from different parts of England and America," he was "a little cast down to find some English friends had thrown aside the use of means" |that is, the means of grace, apparently a reference to those who had joined the Moravians|, while "others were disputing for *sinless perfection* and *universal redemption* ," clearly a reference to the Wesleys. "I know no such things asserted in the gospel, if explained aright."[55] To a friend in New York he wrote that he believed God was calling him back to England, and that "Mr. W— and the M—s |Wesley and the Moravians?|" were "sadly erroneous in some points of doctrine." To another in Britain who had complained that some were teaching "sinless perfection," Whitefield replied that in his view such a state was "unattainable in this life" and that "there is no man that liveth and sinneth not in thought, word, and deed." It was absurd, he added, "to affirm such a thing as perfection, and to deny *final persever-ance.*"[56]

Amidst the great awakening that his preaching in the various Boston congregational churches inspired, Whitefield took time to write directly to John Wesley, in answer to a letter Wesley had written him on March 25, which now has been lost. "I think I have for some time known what it is to have righteousness, peace, and joy in the Holy Ghost," Whitefield began, quoting words of St. Paul (Romans 14:17) that Wesley used constantly to describe what it means to be a child of God. "But I cannot say I am free from indwelling sin. No, I find a law in my members, warring against the law of my mind, that makes me cry out, 'Who shall deliver me from the body of this death?' " (Romans 7:24). These words suggest that the evangelist did not yet comprehend fully, or else chose not to acknowledge, that Wesley was now teaching that deliverance from the inward bent to sinning was promised in a second work of grace, beyond the new birth. He cited then the article in the Anglican creed that Wesley still and always heartily affirmed, declaring inward corruption to remain in those who have experienced regeneration. "I am sorry, honored Sir," Whitefield continued, "to hear by many letters that you seem to own a sinless perfection in this life attainable." On the contrary, he reasoned, the continual struggle with inbred sin is necessary to keep a Christian humble and looking "constantly to Jesus for pardon and forgiveness." True, he acknowledged, many abuse this teaching "and perhaps willfully indulge sin, or do not aspire after holiness." But he could not on that account "assert doctrines contrary to the gospel." Wesley must have been startled to read the words, "I know no sin (except that against the Holy Ghost) that a child of God (if God should withhold his grace) may not be guilty of." Was this, indeed, the same man who had written the sermon on "Marks of the New Birth"?[57]

The letter did not, however, mean that Whitefield had abandoned the teaching both men knew they shared with Pietists, Quakers, and Puritans—that the power of the Holy Spirit enables persons who are truly born again to overcome temptation. Whitefield had simply begun to rely on the doctrines of election and final perseverance to deal with the fact that they often fall into sin, as did King David, whom Scripture had earlier called "a man after God's own heart," and Peter, who denied his Lord. The very next day, however, the evangelist explained to another correspondent what must have been for him a new understanding of the link between a predestined new birth and the assurance of final salvation: "Thus (says Saint Paul) 'those whom He justified, them He also glorified'; so that if a man was once justified, he remains so to all eternity."[58]

The next month, in New York City, Whitefield was confronted by a public letter from some church members of the Presbyterian persuasion, challenging certain passages in the two-volume edition of his early sermons that Benjamin Franklin had brought out a few months before. Whitefield published his answer at once, saying he welcomed the chance "to retract some expressions that have formerly drop'd from my pen, before God was pleased to give me a more clear knowledge of the doctrines of grace." He regretted statements that had said or implied that one who was truly converted could lose his hope of eternal salvation, and for having spoken of being baptized "into the nature" of Christ when he should have said into "the name" of Christ. And he specifically renounced the words, "He that is born again of God sinneth not," that had appeared in his preface to the memoirs of Thomas Haliburton (for an English edition of which John Wesley had also written a preface). Clearly, however, his American audiences, chiefly of Reformed background, were pressing upon him a public separation from "Mr. Wesley in his errors."[59]

Returning south by way of Philadelphia in early November, 1740, Whitefield found in the Quaker city another letter from Wesley, this one written a full eight months earlier. "O that we were of one mind," Whitefield responded. "For I am yet persuaded, you greatly err. You have set a mark you will never arrive at, till you come to glory. . . . O that God may give you a sight of his free, sovereign, and electing love!" Then, pleading friendship, he wrote, "I am willing to go with you to prison and to death; but I am not willing to oppose you. . . . Dear, dear sir, study the covenant of grace, that you may be consistent with yourself."[60]

On Christmas Eve, therefore, at his orphanage in Bethesda, Georgia, Whitefield wrote John Wesley a long letter denouncing his friend's views on both Christian perfection and free grace. At the risk of their friendship, he told Wesley that he would publish the letter in Charleston, Boston, and, on his return, in London. This fateful decision stemmed from what Whitefield thought was the relationship between Wesley's rejection of predestination and his doctrine of Christian perfection. The letter also records the young evangelist's retreat from his once high view of the "sanctifying graces" imparted in the new birth. He acknowledged "with grief and humble shame" that although during the "five or six years" since he had received the "full assurance of faith" he had "not doubted a quarter of an hour of having a saving interest in Jesus Christ," he had often "fallen into sin." He had not been nor did he expect ever to be "able to live one day perfectly free from all defects and sin."[61]

Lumping the last two words together, of course, confused the careful distinction that Wesley had drawn, from the moment he began to preach the promise of cleansing from all sin, between human frailty and a corrupted heart.[62] Worse, Whitefield in the next breath denounced an error that the Wesleys never held, namely "that after a man is born again he cannot commit sin." And in the letter's closing paragraphs he abandoned his customary deference to tell his friend bluntly, "I believe your fighting so strenuously against the doctrine of election, and pleading so vehemently for a sinless perfection, are among the reasons . . . why you are kept out of the liberties of the gospel, and that full assurance of faith which they enjoy who have experimentally tasted and daily feed upon God's electing, everlasting love."[63]

John Wesley, always careful not to claim more grace than he had, stood thus publicly accused by one of his closest associates of not enjoying even a clear experience of regeneration.[64] But the judgment was rooted in Whitefield's conclusion that Scripture taught only one renewing work of the Holy Spirit, the new birth, whereas Wesley was now hungering and thirsting for a second and deeper renewal in God's image. In that sublime moment, Wesley declared for the rest of his life, the underlying impulse to pride, self-will, and anger that persists in every believer's heart (and that he thought represented the "remains of inbred sin") would be entirely cleansed away. Persons thus sanctified would then be able to love God with all their hearts and their neighbors as themselves.[65] Having been preoccupied for fifteen months with resisting the "speculative antinomianism" he thought was implicit in Moravian stillness,[66] Wesley now had to confront similar tendencies in the Calvinist party. Many of that party were far more willing than Whitefield to condone sinning by believers. And they were happy to be able to draw upon Whitefield's letter to accuse John Wesley of teaching salvation by works rather than by grace, and to ground that accusation upon both doctrines in question: unlimited atonement and Christian perfection.

Once having joined the argument against entire sanctification in public print, Whitefield never relented. Late in April, 1741, he responded to a friend (possibly Howell Harris) who had been put off by his statement that there is "no such thing" as dominion over the carnal nature with these words: "We shall never have such a dominion over indwelling sin as entirely to be delivered from the stirring of it." Moreover, Whitefield continued, "the greatest saint cannot be assured but [that] some time or other, for his humiliation or punishment for unfaithfulness, God may permit it to break out into some actual breach of his law, and in a gross way too."[67] To a lady in Edinburgh, recently converted, Whitefield wrote: "What does the Lord require of you now, but to walk humbly with Him? Beg Him to show you more and more of your evil heart, that you may ever remain a poor sinner at the feet of the once crucified but now exalted lamb of God. There you will be happy." Earlier he would have declared, with all the other awakened Methodists, that the Christian's happiness stems from the power to live righteously.[68]

A bit later, Whitefield published an answer to an anonymous tract, attributed to the Bishop of London, entitled *Observations upon the Conduct and Behaviour of. . .Methodists.* The evangelist stoutly defended the doctrine that the new birth is "a *sudden* and *instantaneous* change," in which "the righteousness of *Jesus Christ*" is "imputed and applied to their souls by faith, through the operation of the eternal Spirit." This doctrine he and the Wesleys continued everywhere to declare. But he denied ever imagining that he "had attain'd or was already perfect," or teaching others "to imagine that they were so." On the contrary, he wrote, "I expect to carry a body of sin and death about with me as long as I live."[69]

During the years that followed both Whitefield and John Wesley worked hard to minimize their estrangement. Both men wrote gracious letters which, though reiterating their differences, demonstrated their common opposition to Moravian teaching, affirmed their resistance to antinomianism, and refuted the charge that Wesley had excluded Calvinists from his societies.[70] In his most important theological tract, published in 1745, Wesley declared the charge that he and Whitefield anathematized each other was "grossly, shamelessly false." In every one of the "fundamental doctrines" of Christianity, he said, "we hold one and the same thing. In smaller points, each of us thinks, and lets think. . . . I reverence Mr. Whitefield, both as a child of God, and a true minister of Jesus Christ."[71] In 1748 the evangelist wrote to John Wesley wishing for a union of their followers but regretting that it was not feasible. Wesley's recently-published volumes of sermons demonstrated, he said, "that we differ in principles more that I thought." Moreover, Whitefield's "attachment to America" would not allow him to make long visits to England or to organize his followers into a permanent association of societies, as Wesley had.[72] Whenever he was in Britain, however, Whitefield preached among Wesley's societies, as he put it, "as freely as among those who are called our own."[73]

In 1763, William Warburton, the Anglican bishop of Worcester, wrote a volume deeply critical of the doctrine of the Holy Spirit that both Calvinistic and Wesleyan evangelicals freely proclaimed. Whitefield and John Wesley published closely parallel rejoinders. Both stressed the scriptural promise that the gift of the Holy Spirit in the new birth would empower believers to live a righteous life.[74] Whitefield declared that the "divine tempers" described in Paul's great hymn to Christian love in 1 Corinthians 13 are "flowers not to be gathered in nature's garden. They are exotics; planted originally in heaven, and in the great work of the new birth transplanted by the Holy Ghost, not only into the hearts of the first apostles or primitive Christians but into the hearts of all true believers, even to the end of the world."[75] (The last two phrases had appeared long before in sermons he and Wesley published in 1739 and 1741, the one referring to initial and the other to entire sanctification. The phrases reappeared in 1755 in John Wesley's Notes on Acts 1:5, recording Jesus' promise to his apostles of the baptism with the Holy Spirit.)[76] Whitefield urged that "our earthly hearts do now, and always will, stand in as much need of the quickening, enlivening, transforming influence of the Spirit of Jesus Christ, . . .as the hearts of the first apostles." The Spirit's abiding presence gradually makes "every believer, in every age," truly Christian, he wrote, "by beginning, carrying on, and completing that holiness in the heart and life. . .without which no man living shall see the Lord."[77] Here the language of Whitefield's earliest sermons was revived.[78]

In the closing days of the year 1766, Whitefield wrote a friend praising the Countess Selina, Lady Huntington, for the "single eye" and "disinterested spirit" that marked her "laudable ambition" to lead the Christian vanguard. "O for a plerophory of faith! To be filled with the Holy Ghost," Whitefield exclaimed to his friend. "This is the grand point.

God be praised that you have it in view."[79] Three years later a similar spiritual ambition led John Fletcher, with Wesley's blessing, to accept Lady Huntington's invitation to preside over the founding of Trevecca College. She hoped that at Trevecca the youthful followers of Wesley and Whitefield would unite again, in a love inspired by the Holy Spirit's outpouring.[80]

Little wonder that when news reached England in 1770 that George Whitefield had died and been buried at Newburyport, Massachusetts, John Wesley would allow no one to keep him from fulfilling Whitefield's wish that he preach the memorial sermon in his friend's London pulpit.[81] And in that sermon, before a vast congregation, Wesley proclaimed that these two firebrands of the evangelical movement had never differed on the great doctrine that the gift of the Holy Spirit in the experience of regeneration delivers believers from the power as well as the guilt of sin, enabling them to "walk as Christ also walked."[82]

In retrospect, the research for this book, originally undertaken to find out what Whitefield thought were John Wesley's views, casts new light on many aspects of the younger man's thought and ministry and, accordingly, on the evangelical awakenings in Great Britain and America.

Whitefield's priority is evident in many matters on which he and the Wesleys agreed. He led the way in preaching that in the experience of the new birth the Holy Spirit gives believers deliverance from the dominion of sin. He rooted that proclamation, as the Wesleys always did, in the reformation doctrine of justification—being "made just" by faith. He grounded it, as they did, in what the early church fathers believed was the promise of both the Old and New Testaments: that God's purpose—manifested in Moses and the prophets, in the atonement and resurrection of Christ, and in the pouring out of the sanctifying Spirit at Pentecost—would renew fallen humankind in the divine image of holiness and love. Holiness, for these three and most other leaders of the evangelical awakening, consists in a life of loving God supremely and one's neighbor as oneself, as both Moses and Jesus had taught. That life and the experience of the Holy Spirit's presence makes possible the required growth in holiness, by grace alone, through faith. Moreover, Whitefield pioneered many of the evangelistic measures that the Wesleys and others adopted, such as preaching in the open air, cultivating Anglican fellowship with dissenting ministers and their congregations, and nurturing a sense of common purpose among an interdenominational community of English, Continental, and American evangelicals.

Whitefield's testimony also helps us understand better the origin and substance of the Wesleys' perfectionism, which was, I believe, the more important of the two major points of disagreement between them. Clearly, the central issue was the Wesleyan contention that believers should pray for and expect a second work of sanctifying grace that would cleanse away the "remains of inbred sin." The letters George Whitefield and John Wesley exchanged in 1740 confirm what I earlier concluded on the basis of Wesley's writings: that between July and November, 1739, he and his brother Charles thought they discovered this doctrine of "perfect love" in the Scriptures.[83] I believe that the timing, the scriptural basis, and the moral rigor of this teaching make no longer tenable the notion that John Wesley embraced it only after, and largely because, members of his London and Bristol congregations had begun to profess entire sanctification. The professions followed, they did not precede, the preaching of that promise. Wesleyans proclaimed entire sanctification then and for two centuries afterwards, without diminishing the high doctrine of the new birth that was the hallmark of the evangelical awakening.

Whitefield's writings also bring into clearer focus the character of the New Light Calvinism that he helped colonial pastors to popularize during the revivals of the 1740s. Many parallels between the views of Jonathan Edwards and what Whitefield believed and preached—and, for that matter, some aspects of what Wesley believed and preached—are now apparent. But it is clear that Whitefield's version of covenant theology differed substantially from the stark Augustinian orthodoxy Professor Perry Miller ascribed to Edwards. Rather, what Whitefield nurtured in the American Presbyterian, Congregationalist, and Baptist churches was a renewal of the emphasis that John Calvin and his Puritan heirs had placed on a morally transforming experience of saving grace.[84] Three of Whitefield's earliest sermons on that theme, "The Nature and Necessity of Regeneration," "The Indwelling Spirit, the Common Privilege of All Believers," and "Marks of the New Birth," were published in Boston before he arrived there, and seem to have prompted the near unanimous invitation of the Boston pastors for him to come and preach in their pulpits.

This helps to explain the ease and consistency with which Wesley's perfectionism was exported to America.[85] The ideas that righteousness in both private and public life is the central purpose of redemption, as well as the actual consequence of mass conversions, were never monopolies of Methodists, in either Britain or America. The character of John Wesley's ethics, recently spelled out with great clarity by Leon O. Hynson, was akin to much that was happening in other branches of evangelicalism in the late eighteenth and early nineteenth centuries, though this fact has often escaped the notice of recent scholars, whether Reformed, Pietist, or Wesleyan.[86]

If these conclusions are valid, then they pose important new questions about the cultural history of revolutionary and early national America. The first stage of the long struggle between piety and moralism, between "dead orthodoxy" and the power of righteousness, involved primarily the two parties of Old and New Light Calvinists; Methodists in the United States were few until after 1775.

Francis Asbury's followers, who after their withdrawal from the Anglican Church in 1784 multiplied as rapidly in the cities of Baltimore, Philadelphia, New York, Charleston, and, later, Boston as in the pioneer western settlements, shared fully the New Light moral perspective.[87] That the drive for holiness, and not simply the assurance of salvation, was the governing theme of early Methodism on both sides of the Atlantic is now taken for granted among students of that movement's history, as indeed it was among the first generation of Methodist historians.[88] Neither in England or America did Wesleyans see any way to fulfill their mission to "reform the nation," as the Book of Discipline put it, than "to spread scriptural holiness over these lands."

This larger moral purpose, I think, was the basis of the "evangelical united front" that persisted through most of the nineteenth century, drawing together American Presbyterians, Baptists, Congregationalists, Methodists, the Disciples and Churches of Christ, Peace-Church people, and most of the Lutherans (who were heirs, along with Moravians and Brethren, of the German Pietists). Pioneer Black Methodists and Baptists slowly embraced, though on their own terms, the same moral hopes. These hopes sustained loyalty to the nation and the resistance to slavery and all other forms of oppression that American Blacks have ever since displayed.[89]

Broader aspects of American political and religious history also look different when the moral promise of Whitefield's Reformed evangelicalism is clear. The revolutionary rhetoric calling for "a republic of virtue" may not have owed as much to the fascination of colonial elites with Enlightenment ideals, which Gordon S. Wood argues, as to the widespread conviction that personal rectitude was one of the sure marks of new life in Christ.[90] Mid-nineteenth-century spokespersons for a "righteous empire," whom a generation of recent scholars have scorned for their alleged separation of public and private morality, reflected an admirable if often frustrated effort to unite the two, as I and others have persistently argued.[91] During the early part of that century Unitarians found both popular and intellectual support for their ethical preaching from the growing concern for righteousness in private and public life that Jonathan Edwards had sparked, Whitefield's preaching had kindled, and Francis Asbury and Samuel Hopkins had brought to white heat.

Since colonial days, the idea of moral transformation, through what evangelicals have long called the new birth, has been one of the chief building blocks of American Christianity. The nation's newspaper and magazine publishers have frequently forgotten that fact, as when they breathlessly announced as a new development of the 1970s what was in fact a principal article of the old time religion.

NOTES

1. Albert C. Outler, ed., *John Wesley* (New York, 1964, in a *Library of Protestant Thought*, ed. John Dillenberger and others), "Introduction," 3–34, and 121–3; Martin Schmidt, *John Wesley, A Theological Biography: Volume I* . . . , tr. Norman Goldhawk (New York, London, 1962), 43–53, 73–114; and Timothy L. Smith, "John Wesley and the Wholeness of Scripture," *Interpretation* 39 (July, 1985): 246–62.

2. Schmidt, *Wesley*, I, 23–30. Geoffrey F. Nuttall, *The Holy Spirit in Puritan Faith and Experience* (Oxford, 1946), 4–8, 14–9, 28–33, 42–5, 134–40, and 154–57 illuminates the Puritan and Quaker backgrounds of the evangelical movement; but on the precise distinction between the convicting and evangelically converting work of the Holy Spirit in every person, cf. Hugh Barbour, *The Quakers in Puritan England* (New Haven, 1964), 110–3.

3. F. Ernest Stoeffler, *German Pietism During the Eighteenth Century* (Leyden, 1973); John R. Weinlick, "Moravians in the American Colonies," in F. Ernest Stoeffler, ed., *Continental Pietism and Early American Christianity* (Grand Rapids, Michigan, 1976), 123–34.

Michael R. Watts, *The Dissenters: From the Reformation to the French Revolution* (Oxford, 1978), 394–406, 421–31, 434–45, synthesizes powerfully the recent scholarship on these three impulses to the eighteenth-century awakenings. His account of Wesley's doctrine of Christian perfection, however (pp. 428–29), is awry, apparently from inattention to the central doctrine of prevenient grace. On that theme, see Harald G. A. Lindström, *Wesley and Sanctification: A Study in the Doctrine of Salvation* (Stockholm and London, 1946; Wilmore, Ky.: Francis Asbury Publishing Company, 1982), 44–50. Jean Orcibal, "The Theological Originality of John Wesley and Continental Spirituality," in Rupert E. Davies and Gordon Rupp, eds., *A History of the Methodist Church in Great Britain*, 2 vols. (London, 1965, 1978), I: 81–113, sets Wesley in the context of Roman Catholic as well as Protestant traditions of spirituality.

4. George Whitefield, *A Short Account of God's Dealings with the Reverend Mr. George Whitefield . . . to the Time of His Entering Into Holy Orders* (London, 1740), reprinted, with critical notes, in George Whitefield, *Journals* . . . , ed. Arnold Dallimore (London, 1960), 46–7, 68–9, 77, 80–9, relies on Whitefield's slightly revised text of 1745; John Wesley arranged the publication of the original edition at London early in 1740. For Whitefield's writing of this *Account* aboard ship to Philadelphia, see (in the same place) his journal entries for August 27 and September 8, 1739. Cf. George Whitefield, Gloucester, June 11 and summer 1735, to John Wesley, in George Whitefield, *Letters . . . for the Period 1734–1742* (London, 1976), 483, 485.

Schmidt, *Wesley*, 1:52–58, analyzes Scougal's *Life of God in the Soul of Man* and its impact upon Susanna Wesley and her sons; John Wesley published an abridgment of it at Bristol in 1744.

5. George Whitefield, *A Sermon on Regeneration, Preached to a Numerous Audience in England*, 2nd ed. (Boston: T. Fleet, 1739), printed below, appeared first in London in 1737 under the title stated in the text. Whitefield describes its preparation and reception there in *Short Account*, 86.

6. John Wesley, *Journal*, in his *Works*, ed. Thomas Jackson, 14 vols. (London: 1872; Kansas City, Mo.: Beacon Hill, 1968), entries for January 8, 9, and 24 and May 24, 1738. Charles Wesley, *Journal . . .* , ed. Thomas Jackson, 2 vols. (London, 1849; Kansas City, Mo.: Beacon Hill, 1980), 1:72–9, entries for June–November 1737, show that after his return from Georgia and parallel to his growing acquaintance with the Moravians, Charles was wholly absorbed in seeking, and teaching the doctrine of, the new birth, though he may not have yet conceived it to be experienced instantaneously, by faith, as Peter Böhler convinced the Wesleys it was in the spring of 1738; see the same, 84–7, April and May 1738.

7. Key passages in the two sermons of 1733 appear in Wesley, *Works*, VI:204–5, 209–10, and VII:491. The former appears also in John Wesley, *Sermons* I, 1–33, ed. Albert C. Outler, vol. 1 of *The Works of John Wesley*, ed. Frank Baker (Nashville: Abingdon, 1979), 404–6, 411. Cf. Charles Wesley, *Sermons . . . , with a Memoir of the Author* (London, 1816), discourses that Richard Heitzenrater has recently demonstrated that John Wesley composed no later than the dates indicated: "He That Winneth Souls Is Wise" (July 12, 1731), pp. 13–4, 17; "One Thing Is Needful" (May, 1734), pp. 85–6, 89–91; and "Thou Shalt Love the Lord Thy God" (Sept. 15, 1733), pp. 136–7, 144, 159. Compare John Wesley's other early sermons, "The Christian's Rest" (September 21, 1735), *Works*, VII:367–63; and "On Love" (February 20, 1736), VII:497–8.

8. Whitefield, *Sermon on Regeneration*, 5, 6, 7, 20, 21. Frederick Dreyer, "Faith and Experience in the Thought of John Wesley," *The American Historical Review*, 88 (February 1983), 15–6, misreads the continual Methodist emphasis that "righteousness" is the "ordinary" gift of the Holy Spirit to believers, without which the "emotional reactions or effects" of "peace, love, and joy" bore no witness of salvation at all. That the young evangelist preached this same doctrine during his first stay in Georgia, in 1737 and 1738, is clear from a letter written by George Whitefield on board the "Mary," October 2, 1738, to "The Inhabitants of Savannah," in Whitefield, *Letters . . .* 1734–1742, 491–3.

9. John Wesley, *A Sermon on Salvation by Faith* (London, 1738), 3–4 (also in *Works*, 5:11–12; and in John Wesley, *Sermons* I, 123–5). I have attempted to assign the earliest likely dates of the composition of Wesley's sermons in my article, "Chronological List of John Wesley's Sermons and Doctrinal Essays," *The Wesleyan Theological Journal*, 17 (Fall 1982): 88–110; dates that appear in brackets after the titles of sermons cited below are drawn from that preliminary effort.

10. On the centrality of these evangelical affirmations to John Wesley, see again his *Salvation by Faith*, 9–13; John Wesley, London, March 20, 1739, to James Hervey, in John Wesley, *Letters* I, 1721–1739, ed. Frank Baker, vol. 25 of *The Works of John Wesley*, ed. Frank Baker (New York: Oxford, 1980), 610–1. Cf. the close analysis

of the ecumenical character of early eighteenth-century "spiritual theology" in Richard F. Lovelace, *The American Pietism of Cotton Mather: Origins of American Evangelicalism* (Washington: Christian University, 1979), 3, 33, 35–6, 91–2; and, generally, 251–81.

11. The constancy of this definition of *evangelical* from the eighteenth century to the present is spelled out in my as yet unpublished chapters prepared for a forthcoming volume that I have written jointly with several younger colleagues, *The American Evangelical Mosaic.*

12. Whitefield, *Journals,* December 8, 1738 to March 1, 1739, esp. December 10, February 9–10, and March 1; Wesley, *Journal,* December 11, 1738.

13. Whitefield, *Journals,* February 23, 1739, seems to record Whitefield's earliest consciousness that he was committed to "field preaching," a phrase that referred not to rural fields, of course, but to open spaces in or near the centers of cities and towns; cf. George Whitefield, *A Further Account of God's Dealings . . . from the Time of His Ordination to His Embarking for Georgia (June 1736–December 1737)* (London, 1740), reprinted in Whitefield, *Journals,* 90.

14. Whitefield, *Journals,* March 3, 7–9 and April 4–7, 1739.

15. Wesley, *Journal,* May 25, 1738. Cf. his subsequent entries recounting this search: May 26–29, June 6–7, July 6, October 14, 1738, and January 4, 1739. His intensely pessimistic self-examination of October 14, 1738, should be read in the light of the following: John Wesley, "A Second Letter to the Author of The Enthusiasm of Methodists and Papists Compared" (London, 1750), in *The Appeals to Men of Reason and Religion,* ed. Gerald R. Cragg, vol. 11 in *The Works of John Wesley,* ed. Frank Baker (New York: Oxford, 1975), 402 (also in Wesley, *Works,* 9:36), and his restrained but seemingly clear testimonies to a satisfying witness of the Spirit in a letter from John Wesley, Bristol, May 10, 1739 in Wesley, *Letters* I, 645–6.

16. George Whitefield, Gibraltar, February 27, 1738, to an unidentified person; the same, at sea, April 14, 1738, to Mrs. A. H.; the same, Basingstoke, February 8, 1739, to an unidentified man; and the same, Oxon, April 24 and 27, 1739, to Mrs. H.—; all in George Whitefield, *Letters . . . Written to His Most Intimate Friends, and Persons of Distinction . . . from the Year 1734 to 1770 . . . ,* 3 vols. (London, 1772), 1:39, 40–1, 47–9. See also Whitefield, *Journals,* January 23–24, 1739; cf. February 25 and March 6, 1738.

17. John Wesley's sermons of the same period, "Salvation by Faith" [June 7, 1738], *Works,* 5:11 (also in *Sermons* I, 123–4); "Marks of the New Birth" [April 3, 1741], *Works,* 5:214–16 (also in *Sermons* I, 419–21); and "The Great Privilege of Those That Are born of God" [September 23, 1739], *Works,* 5:227–33 (also in *Sermons* I, 435–41), affirm and explain the nature of that "dominion over sin" that his *Journal* for May 24 (par. 11–12, 16), 25, 27, and 29 declared the preeminent sign of regeneration.

18. I have used the text, apparently reprinted, in George Whitefield, *The Marks of the New Birth; A Sermon Preached at the Parish Church of St. Mary, White-Chapel, London* (London: Printed for C. Whitefield, 1739). Cf. George Whitefield, *Works . . . ,* ed. John Gillies, 6 vols. (London, 1771), 6:161; and Whitefield, *Journals,* January 9 and March 21, 1739. *The National Index of American Imprints* reports a sixth edition published in New York in 1739, and others in Philadelphia in November of that year and in Boston the next year.

19. Whitefield, *Marks of the New Birth*, 5, 8. John Fletcher quoted this sermon at length in his *Last Check to Antinomianism* (1776) to show Whitefield's successors that "before he embraced St. Augustine's mistakes, which are known among us by the name of 'Calvinism,'" Whitefield "was no enemy to Christian perfection, and thought that some had actually attained it"; John Fletcher, *Works*, 4 vols. (Salem, Ohio: Schmul Publishers, 1976), 2:550–1.

20. Whitefield, *Marks of the New Birth*, 11.

21. Charles Wesley's Oxford sermon, "Awake Thou That Sleepest" [April 4, 1742], in John Wesley, *Works*, 5:30–4 (also in *Sermons* I, 149–56), summarized the constant linkage the two brothers made between the gift of the Holy Spirit and the experience of the "new creature" who partakes of the divine nature, precisely as Whitefield did in his *Sermon on Regeneration*, 20–21. Cf. John Wesley, "The First Fruits of the Spirit" [June 25, 1745], *Works*, 5:88–9 (also in *Sermons* I, 235–7); John Wesley, "The Spirit of Bondage and Adoption" [April 25, 1739], 5:105–7 (also in *Sermons* I, 258–62); and Wesley, *Journal*, February 4 and April 8, 1739.

22. Wesley, *Journal*, March 15, 28, 31 and April 1–2, 1739.

23. Ibid., April 1–3, 5, 8; and John Wesley, Bristol, April 9, 1739, to James Hutton, summarizing the first full week of the revival at Bristol, in his *Letters* I, 631–3. The latter was the first of a weekly series to James Hutton that provide an invaluable supplement to the *Journal* for April and May.

24. Whitefield, *Journals*, May 9 and June 3, 1739, records the immense size of his open-air congregations in London, and his visits to Bedford, Hertford, Northampton, and other places; but see especially the "Fourth Journal" for June 4–August 3, 1739, particularly the entries for June 18, July 10–14, and July 21.

25. John Wesley, *Free Grace*, A *Sermon Preach'd at Bristol* (London, 1740); Wesley, *Journal*, April 26, 29, 1739; John Wesley, Bristol, April 26, 1739, to James Hutton, in Wesley, *Letters* I, 635–7; George Whitefield, London, June 25, 1739, and Gloucester, July 2, 1739, to John Wesley, in Whitefield, *Letters . . . , 1734–1742*, 497, 499 (also in Wesley, *Letters* I, 611–2, 667); and, for Whitefield's continuing admiration for John Wesley's work in Bristol and that of Charles in London, see Whitefield, *Journals*, April 30 and July 7 and 21, 1739. Wesley never reissued the sermon, and did not include it in any collection of his writings. See Wesley, *Works*, 7:363, for the editor's comment; and for the offending sermon, see pp. 373–86.

26. The quotation is from Whitefield, *Journals*, May 28, 1739. Cf. George Whitefield, Bristol, July 9, 1739, to the Bishop of Gloucester, in the same, July 9, 1739.

27. Whitefield, *Journals*, March 24, 25, and 28, and May 9 and 13, 1739. The entry for July 11, 1738 indicates the likelihood that the orphanage that Salzburger Pietists had established in Georgia inspired his plan to build one at Savannah.

28. Whitefield, *Journals*, April 21, 22 (containing his letter dated April 22, 1739 to Charles Kinchin), and 25; and Wesley, *Journal*, June 6, 1738, recording the first of his many sensible responses to this Moravian notion.

29. George Whitefield, Blendon, June 12, 1739, to an unnamed society, in Whitefield, *Letters*, 1:50; Wesley, *Journal*, January 28 and June 22, 1739. Cf. John Wesley, Bristol, June 7, 1739, to James Hutton, *Letters* I, 658; and Hillel Schwartz, *The French Prophets: The History of a Millenarian Group in Eighteenth-Century England* (Berkeley, 1980), 311–8.

30. Wesley, *Journal*, July 6, 12, 1739; Cf. George Whitefield, *The Indwelling of the Spirit, the Common Privilege of All Believers. A Sermon Preached at the Parish Church of Bexly, in Kent, on Whitsunday*, 1739 (London, 1739). *The National Index of American Imprints* lists a Boston edition in 1739 and others at Philadelphia and Williamsburg in 1740. Cf. Nuttall, *Holy Spirit*, references above, note 2.

31. Whitefield, *Indwelling of the Spirit*, 5; the quotations here and later in the paragraph all agree with his slightly revised version in *Twenty-three Sermons on Various Subjects . . .*, new ed. (London, 1745). Cf. Whitefield, *Journals*, May 28 and July 12, 1739; and Lovelace, *Mather*, 50–2, 91–7, 185–7.

32. Whitefield, *Indwelling of the Spirit*, 13–18, the quotations being on 17 and 18.

33. George Whitefield, *The Power of Christ's Resurrection: A Sermon Preached at Werburgh's in the City of Bristol* (London, 1739), 10. For an example of Whitefield's strong language about the inward sanctification of the "true Christian," see pp. 11–13.

34. Alan Heimert, *Religion and the American Mind: From the Great Awakening to the Revolution*, (Cambridge: Harvard University, 1966), 34–39, links Whitefield's doctrine of the new birth more closely to Calvinism than the evidence that he cites justifies.

35. The Moravian challenge was a long-standing and persistent one; see Wesley, *Journal*, June 6, 1738, November 1, 4, 7–10 and December 13, 19, 31, 1739, and April 23, 25, 30 and June 22–24, 1740; and John Wesley, Oxford, November 17, 1738 to Benjamin Ingham and James Hutton, in Wesley, *Letters* I, 580. Wesley's elaborate account of his own experience after Aldersgate as a "babe in Christ" who was "weak in the faith"—as well as his lengthy report of what he heard at Herrnhut in August, 1738—was composed after the crisis in the Fetter Lane Society in London had reached its height, and was printed in September, 1740. It may have been shaped by his need to counter Moravian arguments.

36. Wesley, *Journal*, July 21–23 and October 9 and 19, 1739; cf. his references to explaining the nature of Christian holiness (apparently to society meetings) in the entries for September 13, October 1, 3, 7, 10, and 15, 1739. Cf. the entries for August 1 and 12, 1738 for Wesley's account of Moravian Christian David's exposition of the Sermon on the Mount at Herrnhut, written up for publication of that section of Wesley's *Journal* in 1740. It seems to me that this passage reflects Wesley's perspective on that sermon and related testimonies in the latter year.

37. John Wesley, "Sermon on the Mount—Discourse III" [July 26, 1739], *Works*, 5:278–79, 280–5, 293 (also in *Sermons* I, 510–1, 513–20, 530).

38. John Wesley, "Diary," printed parallel to his *Journal*, ed. Nehemiah Curnock, 8 vols. (London: Epworth, 1909–16). The entries for November 7–8, 1739, record that he wrote *Christian Perfection* and "writ Law." Richard Heitzenrater believes both refer to his condensation of *The Nature and Design of Christianity* (London, 1740), discussed in Frank Baker's ms. bibliography of Wesley's writings under item 41, pp. 265–8. But that condensation deals with the whole of the "great salvation," not with the experience of perfect love. Wesley, *Journal*, November 17 (quoted here) is echoed in the entry for August 10, 1740, where he uses his famous sermon's text, Philippians 3:12, to urge believers to "press forward for the prize of their high calling, even a clean heart. . . ."

I have examined A *Practical Treatise on Christian Perfection* . . . (Newcastle, 1743). It treats that achievement (pp. 1–16) just as Wesley and Whitefield had been expounding it before the fall of 1739—as a part of the whole work of God in the soul that begins in the new birth. Law had long since taught the Holy Club to affirm this. Wesley may have reviewed and edited this work in the process of discovering where exactly he had taken a position based on, but beyond, Law's. Certainly Law's chapters 3 and 4, on the Christian's duty to self-denial (pp. 32–64), were a powerful answer to Moravian claims, and undergirded Wesley's advance over Law. But the book does not touch on one of the matters then concerning Wesley—that of a second "moment" of sanctifying grace. So the cryptic words in the "Diary" for November 7 and 8 seem likely to refer to both a first draft of his sermon and his first work on *Nature and Design of Christianity*.

39. Wesley, *Journal*, entries for January 9 and 15, March 5 and 28, April 14, May 5, June 1 and 24, and August 1, 1740.

40. My article, "The Holy Spirit in the Hymns of the Wesleys," *The Wesleyan Theological Journal*, 17 (Summer, 1981):28, pays special attention to this earliest published description of the experience of entire sanctification, namely John Wesley's preface to the second volume of Charles and John Wesley, *Hymns and Sacred Poems* (London, 1740), which appears in his *Works*, 14:322–7.

41. John Wesley, *A Plain Account of Christian Perfection* . . . (London, 1766; also in *Works*, 11:378–81). Wesley misdated this hymnbook as 1741 in the *Plain Account* and accordingly gave priority there to his essay on *The Character of a Methodist* (London, 1742) and his sermon, *Christian Perfection* (London, 1741), though both were published after the hymnbook; see the discussion in my article, "The Holy Spirit in the Hymns of the Wesleys," 28–9.

42. George Whitefield, London, August 3, 1739, to an unnamed Scottish clergyman, in Whitefield, *Letters*, 1:58.

43. I have used the text of the original edition (London, 1739), where these quotations appear on pp. 3, 10–11. These Scripture citations appear to be Philippians 3:12, 15; Genesis 17:1; Deuteronomy 18:13; and Matthew 5:48. Cf. Whitefield, *Journals*, April 29, 1739; and Arnold A. Dallimore, *George Whitefield: The Life and Times of the Great Evangelist of the Eighteenth-Century Revival*, 2 vols. (London, 1970, 1980), 1:197, 224, 316, 404–9. Dallimore was so absorbed with the early signs of Whitefield's developing Calvinism that he did not comment at all on these deep and long-standing agreements with the Wesleys.

44. Whitefield, *Short Account*, 71 (where these words from the 1740 edition appear alongside a revision and extension of them in his later editions); and, generally, 47, 51–52, 54–55, 59, 60, 84, 90. George Whitefield, Philadelphia ["wrote at sea"], November 8, 1739, to John Wesley, in Wesley, *Letters* 1, 698–9, requested Wesley to publish his *Short Account*, and reported lovingly that his close reading of Puritan authors had confirmed his Calvinist convictions.

45. Whitefield, *Journals*, August 25 and September 8, 1739. Cf. entries for August 31 and September 22, 1739.

46. Ibid., September 29 and 30, 1739. Cf. November 4, 1739, for a parallel observation on Quaker preaching.

47. Ibid., October 13, 1739. Dallimore, *Whitefield*, 1:401–9, argued strenuously that the evangelist's journal and correspondence show that he became a full-blown Calvinist during this voyage as a result of reading Calvinist theological tracts in the light of his own severe self-examination. But the statements that Dallimore quoted (pp. 406–8) do not seem to me different from Whitefield's language of the previous years, and no more "Calvinist" in their insistence that good works follow and depend upon regeneration than Wesley had been since Aldersgate.

48. Whitefield, *Journals*, November 27 (for the quotation), October 30, and November 8, 10, 13–8, 20, 22, and 29–30, 1739; Weinlick, "Moravianism in the American Colonies," in Stoeffler, ed., *Continental Pietism and Early American Christianity*, 134–9; Martin H. Schrag, "The Impact of Pietism Upon the Mennonites in early American Christianity," ibid., 74–87. Evidence of a long debate between Quakers and Brethren over the nature of the baptism of the Spirit is found in the anonymous work, *A Humble Gleam of the Despised Little Light of Truth* . . . (Philadelphia, 1747), reprinted in Donald F. Durnbaugh, ed., *The Brethren in Colonial America* (Elgin, Ill., 1967), 434, 439–40, 442, 445–6.

49. Whitefield, *Journals*, November 25, 1739 and October 12, 1740; Whitefield, "The Lord Our Righteousness," in George Whitefield, *Nine Sermons Upon the Following Subjects; Viz. The Lord our Righteousness. . . . Christ: The Believers Wisdom, Righteousness, Sanctification and Redemption* . . . . (Edinburgh, 1742), 1–26.

50. For direct parallels with Whitefield's points cited below, see John Wesley, *The Lord Our Righteousness* (London, 1766) [which I have concluded he preached as early as October 22, 1758], in *Works*, 5:239–42, 244 (also in *Sermons* I, 455–60, 462–3).

51. Whitefield, "The Lord Our Righteousness," in Whitefield, *Nine Sermons*, 8, 18. Cf. p. 302, on the opening lines of the Sermon on the Mount, with John Wesley, "Sermon on the Mount—Discourse I" and "Discourse II" [July 21, 1739], in *Works*, 5:256, 267–9 (also in *Sermons* I, 480, 495–8). See also Whitefield, *Journals*, January 9, 1740, quoting a Wesley poem of prayer for the coming of the "Spirit of refining fire."

52. Whitefield, *Journals*, show the sharp contrast between opposition from colonial Anglican pastors and support from dissenting ones in Philadelphia, New York, Charleston, Providence, and Boston; see entries for November 8–10, 14–7, 20, and 22, 1739, and April 23 and 29, May 1 and 11, July 13, August 25, and September 19, 1740.

53. Whitefield, *Journals*, November 14, 1739 and September 25 and November 5, 1740.

Dallimore, *Whitefield*, 1:405, seems to me correct in minimizing the influence of Jonathan Edwards and other New Englanders on Whitefield's developing Calvinism, for Whitefield did not meet any of them until September, 1740. Moreover, his *Journals*, October 17–19, 1740, recording his visit to Northampton, indicate no significant doctrinal discussion or reflection. But Dallimore underestimated the influence of the Calvinist clergy in the middle and southern colonies upon him.

54. George Whitefield, Savannah, March 26, 1740, to John Wesley, in Whitefield, *Letters*, 1:155–7 (also in John Wesley, *Letters* II, 1740–1755, ed. Frank Baker, vol. 26 in *The Works of John Wesley*, ed. Frank Baker [New York: Oxford, 1982, p. 111]); Whitefield, Cape-Lopen, May 24, 1740, to John Wesley, ibid., 1:181–2. Cf. Whitefield, Savannah, June 25, 1740, and Charles-Town [South Carolina], August 25, 1740, to John Wesley, ibid., 1:189–90, 204–5; and John Wesley, London, August 9, 1740, to George Whitefield, in Wesley, *Letters* II, 31—all in a friendly spirit, and urging avoidance of public controversy over the issues of predestination and final perseverance.

55. Whitefield, *Journals*, September 20, 1740.

56. George Whitefield, Boston, September 23, 1740, to "Mr. N., at New York" and George Whitefield, Boston, September 23, 1740, to "Mr. A.," in Whitefield, *Letters*, 1:208–209.

57. George Whitefield, Boston, September 25, 1740, to "The Rev. Mr. J.W.," ibid., 1:210–2 (quoted here from the more accurate text in Wesley, *Letters* II, 31–33).

58. George Whitefield, Boston, September 26, 1740, to "Mr. I.," Whitefield, *Letters*, 1:213–4. Whitefield's radical doctrine of the Holy Spirit's gift of sanctifying grace in regeneration, published in 1737 in his *Sermon on Regeneration*, 5–7, 20–21, and in 1739 in *The Power of Christ's Resurrection*, 10–12, had commended him to the Boston clergy. Cf. Gillies, *Memoirs of George Whitefield*, 48, for William Seward's report that at a German settlement near Philadelphia on April 24, 1740, Whitefield pressed poor sinners to "claim all their privileges" in Christ, "not only righteousness and peace, but joy in the Holy Ghost." Afterward, Seward wrote, "our dear friend, Peter Böhler, preached in Dutch, to those who could not understand Mr. Whitefield in English."

59. George Whitefield, A *Letter* . . . *to Some Church Members of Presbyterian Persuasion* . . . [dated "New York, Nov. 1, 1740"] (Boston, 1740), 6, 9, 10.

60. George Whitefield, Philadelphia, November 9, 1740, to John Wesley, Whitefield, *Letters*, 1:219, quoted here from the more accurate version in Wesley, *Letters* II, 43.

61. George Whitefield, A *Letter to the Reverend Mr. John Wesley: In Answer to His Sermon, Entitled, Free Grace* (London, 1741), 11–12, 17, 19 (also in Dallimore, *Whitefield*, 2:551–69). Charles Wesley, Bristol, December 3, to John Wesley, in Wesley, *Letters* II, 43–4, demonstrates the intensity of the crisis over Calvinism at this time.

62. The classic case is the sermon "Christian Perfection," in Wesley, *Works*, 6:2–6.

63. Whitefield, *Letter to* . . . *John Wesley*, 19, 20. Cf. Joseph Humphreys, Deptford, February 26, 1741, and May 7, 1741, to John Wesley, in Wesley, *Letters* II, 52, 62–63, for the close link that Wesley's Calvinist followers in Britain perceived between his opposition to predestination and his advocacy of Christian perfection.

64. Wesley, *Journal*, entry for Sunday, February 1, 1741, shows that someone had distributed at the door of his London chapel printed copies of a Whitefield letter, which Frank Baker's yet unpublished research establishes was the one

written to Wesley from Boston on September 25, 1740. Wesley declared he believed that Whitefield had not authorized its publication and invited the congregation to join him in tearing up their copies of it. Wesley's subsequent dismay at the publication of Whitefield's open letter appears in the same, March 28 and April 4. Cf. George Whitefield [on board the *Minerva*], February 1, 1741, to John and Charles Wesley, in Whitefield, *Letters . . . 1734–1742*, 507, a portion of which is also in Wesley, *Letters* II, 48–49.

65. See the discussion and citations above at notes 37–41. Cf. John Wesley, *Scripture Way of Salvation* (London, 1765), which I believe was composed as early as May 22, 1758 (also in Wesley, *Works*, 6:45–46, 50); and John Wesley "On Perfection," which I believe was composed on March 29, 1761 and preached repeatedly thereafter (also in Wesley, *Works*, 6:412–6, 418–9; John Wesley, "Minutes" of the Fourth Annual Conference, for June 17, 1747, in Albert Outler, *John Wesley* (New York: Oxford, 1964), 167–72; John Wesley, A *Plain Account of Genuine Christianity* (Dublin, 1753), quoted in Outler, *Wesley*, 181–91; and John Wesley, "Thoughts on Christian Perfection," from *Sermons on Several Subjects* (London, 1760), quoted in Outler, *Wesley*, 283–98.

66. The conception is an organizing principle in Bernard Semmel, *The Methodist Revolution* (New York, 1973). Cf. [John and Charles Wesley,] *Hymns on God's Everlasting Love, To Which is Added, The Cry of a Reprobate and The Horrible Decree* (Bristol, 1741), reprinted in their *Poetical Works*, ed. G. Osborn, 13 vols. (London, 1869), 3:1–138; and Osborn's "Preface," xiii–xx, arguing the conciliatory character of these hymns.

Whitefield, of course, shared completely Wesley's view of the errors of Moravian "stillness," and returned to England as intent on drawing his admirers away from it as on resisting Wesley's doctrine of heart purity; see his summary of both issues in George Whitefield, on board the *Minerva*, February 20, 1741, "to T — K —, at London," in Whitefield, *Letters*, 1:251–3.

67. George Whitefield, Bristol, April 28, 1741, "to Mr. H — H —," Whitefield, *Letters*, 1:259–60. Harris remained for a long time, as Whitefield's letter put it, "tinctured with the doctrine of sinless perfection." Cf. Wesley, *Journal*, October 9, 10, and 17, 1741; George Whitefield, Aberdeen, October 10, 1741, to John Wesley, in Wesley, *Letters* II, 67; and John Wesley, London, August 6, 1742, to Howell Harris, in Wesley, *Letters* II, 85.

68. George Whitefield, Edinburgh, December 24, 1742, "to Miss S —," Whitefield, *Letters* II, 5–6, with quotation above, note 20.

69. George Whitefield, An *Answer to the First and Second Part of an Anonymous Pamphlet Entitled "Observations Upon the . . . Methodists" in Two Letters to the . . . Bishop of London* (London, 1744), 9; on the new birth, see ibid., 10, 12 (for the quotation), and 17–19. Resistance to the antinomian party of Calvinists became a hallmark of Whitefield's followers; Gillies, *Memoirs of George Whitefield*, 120, shows the evangelist's defenders arguing in 1748 that, despite his earlier extreme statements about the "spiritual assurance" of salvation, Whitefield for the past two years had insisted "that a holy life is the best evidence of a gracious state."

70. See Whitefield's letters to Wesley as follows: Aberdeen, October 10, 1741, and Edinburgh, October 11, 1742, in Whitefield, *Letters*, 1:331, 448–9, (also in

Wesley, *Letters* II, 67, 87); and London, December 21, 1742, in Wesley, *Letters* II, 97–98. Cf. Wesley, *Journal*, August 24, 1742; and his identification with John Calvin's view of justification in John Wesley, Londonderry, May 14, 1765, to John Newton, in Outler, *John Wesley*, 78.

Charles Wesley, |London|, March 16–17, 1741, and Bristol, September 28, 1741, to John Wesley, in Wesley, *Letters* II, 54, 65–6, reveal the younger brother's sharper judgment of Whitefield. But Charles Wesley, Sheffield, October 8, 1749, to Ebenezer Blackwell, records the great and public reconciliation of the three men at Newcastle and Leeds in September, 1749, in Charles Wesley, *Journal . . .* , 1:178.

71. John Wesley, A *Farther Appeal to Men of Reason and Religion, Part I* (London, 1745), in Baker, ed., *The Works of John Wesley*, 11:173 (also in Wesley, *Works*, 8:108).

72. George Whitefield, London, September 1, 1748, to John Wesley, in Wesley, *Letters* II, 327–8.

73. George Whitefield, London, March 5, 1758, to "Professor F —," Whitefield, *Letters*, 3:230. Cf. Gillies, *Whitefield*, 132–3.

74. John Wesley, A *Letter to the Right Reverend the Lord Bishop |Warburton| of Gloucester; Occasioned by His Tract*, "*On the Office and Operations of the Holy Spirit*" (London, 1763), in Baker, ed., *The Works of John Wesley*, 11:505–8, 525–6 (also in Wesley, *Works*, 9:150–3, 165–71); George Whitefield, *Observations on Some Fatal Mistakes . . . |in Dr. William Warburton's| "The Doctrines of Grace; or, The Office and Operations of the Holy Spirit"* . . . (London and Edinburgh, 1764), 16, which heaps scorn on Warburton's attack upon Wesley.

75. Whitefield, *Observations*, 10.

76. Whitefield, *Marks of the New Birth*, 5; Wesley, "Christian Perfection," in *Works*, 6:11.

77. Whitefield, *Observations*, 16.

78. My cursory reading of *The Christian's Magazine*, published by Whitefield's followers in London, yielded several examples of similar language: anon., "On Purity of Heart," *The Christian's Magazine* 5 (September, October, November 1764):385, 387, 433–5, 483 (in the opening section of a long series summarizing "Systematical Divinity"); and J.K., "Thoughts on Christian Perfection" |signed January 8, 1764|, *The Christian's Magazine* 5 (|April?| 1765):600–604.

79. George Whitefield, London, December 30, 1766, to "W — P —, Esq.," and Whitefield, London, December 14, 1768, to the same, in Whitefield, *Letters*, 3:342–3, 379; he affirms in the latter his "moderate Calvinism."

80. I have summarized the evidence in "How John Fletcher Became the Theologian of Wesleyan Perfectionism," *Wesleyan Theological Journal* 15 (Spring 1980):70–71. Cf. Whitefield's comments on his visit to Trevecca, August 26, 1768, in his *Letters*, 3:373–4.

81. Wesley, *Journal*, November 10 and 18, 1772.

82. John Wesley, *On The Death of the Rev. Mr. George Whitefield . . . November 18, 1770* (London, 1770), *Works*, VI, 178–9.

83. See above, notes 38–41.

84. Gregory S. Clapper, " 'True Religion' and the Affections: A Study of John Wesley's Abridgment of Jonathan Edwards' *Treatise on Religious Affections*," *Wesleyan Theologican Journal*, 19 (Fall 1984): 78–79, 82–6, supplements Outler, *John Wesley*, 16.

Edwards' early sermon, "A Divine and Supernatural Light, Immediately Imparted to the Soul by the Spirit of God, Shown to be Both a Scriptural and Rational Doctrine," in his *Works*, 2 vols. (London, 1840), 2:12–14, 17 is the place to begin.

85. Timothy L. Smith, "The Transfer of Wesleyan Religious Culture From England to America," World Methodist Historical Society, *Historical Bulletin*, 14 (First Quarter 1985):2–16. Asbury published "An Account of . . . Joseph Everett . . . ," in *The Arminian Magazine* |Philadelphia|, 2 (October, 1790):505–11, telling of his conversion under new-light Presbyterian preachers, who convinced him that he must be born again, that "religion was the work of an Almighty Power," and that "it was a new creation in the soul" through which "the Divine Spirit" would help him to "break off" from all his sins (p. 507).

86. Leon O. Hynson, *To Reform the Nation: Theological Foundations of Wesley's Ethics* (Grand Rapids, Mich.: Zondervan, 1984), 114–21.

87. Nathan Bangs, *The Errors of Hopkinsianism Detected and Refuted, in Six Letters to the Reverend S|eth| Williston* (New York, 1815).

88. See generally M. Douglas Meeks, ed., *The Future of the Methodist Theological Traditions* (Nashville: Kingswood, 1985), containing the addresses and working papers presented at the Seventh Oxford Institute of Methodist Theological Studies.

89. Timothy L. Smith, "Slavery and Theology: The Emergence of Black Christian Consciousness in Nineteenth-Century America," *Church History*, 31 (December, 1972):497–512.

90. Gordon S. Wood, *The Creation of the American Republic*, 1776–1787 (Chapel Hill, N.C., 1969), 91–124.

91. And as a student once devoted to the opposite view is now arguing: see Jean Miller Schmidt, "Reexamining the Public-Private Split: Reforming the Continent and Spreading Scriptural Holiness," in Russell E. Richey and Kenneth E. Rowe, eds., *Rethinking Methodist History: A Bicentennial Historical Consultation* (Nashville, 1985), 75–90.

WHITEFIELD'S ACCOUNT OF HIS CONVERSION

(from the *Journals* of George Whitefield)

INTRODUCTION

The long description Whitefield wrote of his conversion is much less well known than the parallel one that John Wesley published about himself a year later. It is presented here in its original form, as it appeared in the youthful evangelist's *Short Account of God's Dealings with . . . George Whitefield*. He sent the manuscript to Wesley to publish when he landed in Philadelphia in October 1739, a sign that they were still working together closely. It appeared almost at once in several American editions. A few years later, Whitefield revised the publication, clarifying or taking out passages that had excited what he thought were unfair criticisms. He also changed the text in several points so as to emphasize the Calvinism to which he became more strongly wedded during the widespread revivals he led on that second journey to America. The revised *Short Account* was published in 1756. The text of 1740, printed below, did not reappear in print until William Wale issued it in London in 1905.

The text gives us a remarkable glimpse of the deference that Englishmen not born to one of the favored classes felt toward those who were—in this case, that Whitefield felt toward the Wesleys. It also makes plain the willingness of Oxford University to open its doors to poorer students, through appointing them servants to the others. And it shows the depth of religiosity that was growing in provincial towns like Gloucester and that helped nurture Whitefield's sense of spiritual need well before he went to Oxford.

The passage also reveals the life of the Holy Club in great detail, particularly the willingness of the two Wesleys to be counselors to searching souls and guide their reading. Not only were William Law's books (entitled *A Practical Treatise Upon Christian Perfection* and *A Plain and*

Serious Call to a Devout and Holy Life, published in 1726 and 1729) influential among them, but Charles Wesley himself was responsible for giving Whitefield such volumes as Scottish Presbyterian Henry Scougal's *The Life of God in the Soul of Man* and German Pietist August Francke's treatise *Against the Fear of Man*. The passage also makes it evident that Charles and John Wesley taught Whitefield to seek for a life-transforming experience, which he was soon to begin calling the new birth, without realizing, apparently, that they were themselves relying more upon their obvious piety and good works as marks of conversion than upon an experience of faith.

Despite its occasional extravagance, Whitefield's *Short Account* shows his theological maturity when, as a young evangelist aboard ship on his second journey to America, he wrote down his memory of this experience. His description of an Oxford undergraduate laying aside the habits of his old life in order to find eternal life, and of the extremes to which he finally went in disclaiming reliance upon such abstinence to save him, are all classically Christian. The crucial point came when John Wesley taught him that self-denial, practicing Christian virtue, prayer, fasting, doing good to the bodies of troubled persons, and partaking of the sacraments—what Whitefield called his "externals"—are indeed signs that God's Spirit is working in one's heart, though they provide neither the marks of saving grace nor merits by which to secure it. One must be saved by faith in Christ alone.

Even before their coming to the assurance of faith during Pentecost season, 1738, then, the Wesleys distinguished clearly between close discipleship and the experience of salvation. Although they seem not to have applied it to themselves until after the disappointments of their trip to Georgia, they had the general doctrine of the new birth straight long before John Wesley met the Moravians. What Wesley learned from Peter Böhler, the Moravian preacher, was precisely what his journal tells us plainly enough: that Böhler guided him to the teaching of the Book of the Acts that the experience of saving grace imparts both the assurance of forgiveness and dominion over sin, and that this experience is to be received by grace, in an *instant* of faith in Christ.

❖　❖　❖

Being now near eighteen years old, it was judged proper for me to go to the university. God had sweetly prepared my way. The friends before applied to recommended me to the master of Pembroke College. Another friend took up £10 upon bond, which I have since repaid, to defray the first expense of entering, and the master, contrary to all expectations, admitted me |as a| servitor immediately.

Soon after my admission I went and resided |at the college|, and found my having been used to a public house was now of service to me. For many of the servitors being sick at my first coming up, by my diligent and ready attendance I ingratiated myself into the gentlemens' favor so far that many, who had it in their power, chose me to be their servitor.

This much lessened my expense; and indeed, God was so gracious that with the profits of my place and some little presents made me by my kind tutor, for almost the first three years I did not put all my relations together to above £24 expense. And it has often grieved my soul to see so many young students spending their substance in extravagant living and thereby entirely unfitting themselves for the prosecution of their studies.

I had not been long at the University before I found the benefit of the foundation I had laid in the country for a holy life. I was quickly solicited to join in their excess of riot with several who lay in the same room. God, in answer to prayers before put up, gave me grace to withstand them; and once in particular, it being cold, my limbs were so benumbed by sitting alone in my study because I would not go out amongst them that I could scarce sleep all night. But I soon found the benefit of not yielding; for when they perceived they could not prevail, they let me alone as a singular odd fellow.

All this while I was not fully satisfied of the sin of playing at cards and reading plays, till God upon a fast day was pleased to convince me. For, taking a play to read a passage out of it to a friend, God struck my heart with such power that I was obliged to lay it down again; and, blessed be His Name, I have not read any such book since.

Before I went to the university, I met with Mr. Law's *Serious Call to a Devout Life* but had not then money to purchase it. Soon after my coming up to the university, seeing a small edition of it in a friend's hand, I soon procured it. God worked powerfully upon my soul, as He has since upon many others, by that and his other excellent treatise upon *Christian Perfection*.

I now began to pray and sing psalms thrice every day, besides morning and evening, and to fast every Friday, and to receive the sacrament at a parish church near our college and at the castle, where the despised Methodists used to receive once a month.

The young men so called were then much talked of at Oxford. I had heard of and loved them before I came to the university and so strenuously defended them when I heard them reviled by the students that they began to think that I also in time should be one of them.

For above a twelvemonth my soul longed to be acquainted with some of them, and I was strongly pressed to follow their good example when I saw them go through a ridiculing crowd to receive the Holy Eucharist at St. Mary's. At length, God was pleased to open a door. It happened that a poor woman in one of the workhouses had attempted to cut her throat but was happily prevented. Upon hearing of this, and knowing that both the Mr. Wesleys were ready to every good work, I sent a poor apple-woman of our college to inform Mr. Charles Wesley of it, charging her not to discover who sent her. She went, but contrary to my orders, told my name. He having heard of my coming to the castle and a parish-church sacrament, and having met me frequently walking by myself, followed the woman when she was gone away and sent an invitation to me by her to come to breakfast with him the next morning.

I thankfully embraced the opportunity and, blessed be God, it was one of the most profitable visits I ever made in my life. My soul, at that time, was athirst for some spiritual friends to lift up my hands when they hung down and to strengthen my feeble knees. He soon discovered it and, like a wise winner of souls, made all his discourses tend that way. And when he had put into my hands Professor [August] Francke's treatise *Against the Fear of Man* and a book entitled *The Country Parson's Advice to His Parishioners* (the last of which was wonderfully blessed to my soul), I took my leave.

In a short time he let me have another book, entitled *The Life of God in the Soul of Man*; and though I had fasted, watched and prayed, and received the Sacrament so long, yet I never knew what true religion was till God sent me that excellent treatise by the hands of my never-to-be-forgotten friend. At my first reading it, I wondered what the author meant by saying "that some falsely placed religion in going to church, doing hurt to no one, being constant in the duties of the closet, and now and then reaching out their hands to give alms to their poor neighbors." "Alas," thought I, "if this be not true religion, what is?" God soon showed me; for in reading a few lines further that "true religion was union of the soul with God and Christ formed within us," a ray of divine light was instantaneously darted in upon my soul; and from that moment, but not till then, did I know that I must be a new creature.

Upon this, like the woman of Samaria when Christ revealed Himself to her at the well, I had no rest in my soul till I wrote letters to my relations telling them there was such a thing as the new birth. I imagined they would have gladly received it. But alas, my words seemed to them as idle tales. They thought that I was going beside myself, and by their letters confirmed me in the resolutions I had taken not to go down into the country but continue where I was, lest that by any means the good work which God had begun in my soul might be made of none effect.

From time to time Mr. Wesley permitted me to come unto him and instructed me as I was able to bear it. By degrees he introduced me to the rest of his Christian brethren. They built me up daily in the knowledge and fear of God and taught me to endure hardness like a good soldier of Jesus Christ.

I now began, like them, to live by rule and to pick up the very fragments of my time, that not a moment of it might be lost. Whether I ate or drank or whatsoever I did, I endeavored to do all to the glory of God. Like them having no weekly sacrament, although the rubric required it at our own college, I received every Sunday at Christ Church. I joined with them in keeping the stations by fasting Wednesdays and Fridays and left no means unused which I thought would lead me nearer to Jesus Christ. Regular retirement, morning and evening, at first I found some difficulty in submitting to, but it soon grew profitable and delightful. As I grew ripe for such exercises, I was from time to time engaged to visit the sick and the prisoners and to read to poor people, till I made it a custom, as most of us did, to spend an hour every day in doing acts of charity.

The course of my studies I soon entirely changed. Whereas before I was busied in studying the dry sciences and books that went no further than the surface, I now resolved to read only such as entered into the heart of religion and which led me directly into an experimental knowledge of Jesus Christ, and Him crucified. The lively oracles of God were my soul's delight. The book of the divine laws was seldom out of my hands. I meditated therein day and night; and ever since that, God has made my way signally prosperous and given me abundant success.

God enabled me to do much good to many as well as to receive much from the despised Methodists, and made me instrumental in converting one who is lately come into the Church and, I trust, will prove a burning and shining light.

Several short fits of illness was God pleased to visit and to try me with after my first acquaintance with Mr. Wesley. My new convert was a help-meet for me in those and in all other circumstances, and in company with him and several other Christian friends did I spend many sweet and delightful hours. Never did persons, I believe, strive more earnestly to enter in at the strait gate. They kept their bodies under even to an extreme. They were dead to the world and willing to be accounted as the dung and offscouring of all things, so that they might win Christ. Their hearts glowed with the love of God, and they never prospered so much in the inward man, as when they had all manner of evil spoken against them falsely without.

Many came amongst them for a while who, in time of temptation, fell away. The displeasure of a tutor or head of a college, the changing of a gown from a lower to a higher degree— above all, a thirst for the praise of men more than that which cometh from God and a servile fear of contempt—caused numbers that had set their hand to the plough shamefully to look back. The world, and not themselves, gave them the title of Methodists, I suppose, from their custom of regulating their time and planning the business of the day every morning. Mr. John and Charles Wesley were two of the first that thus openly dared to confess Christ, and they, under God, were the spiritual fathers of most of them. They had the pleasure of seeing the work of the Lord prosper in their hands before they went to Georgia. Since their return, the small grain of mustard-seed has sprung up apace. It has taken deep root. It is growing into a great tree. Ere long, I trust, it will fill the land, and numbers of souls will come from the East and from the West, from the North and from the South, and lodge under the branches of it.

But to return. Whilst I was thus comforted on every side, by daily conversing with so many Christian friends, God was pleased to permit Satan to sift me like wheat, a general account of which I shall, by the Divine assistance, give in the following section. . . .

At my first setting out, in compassion to my weakness, I grew in favor both with God and man and used to be much lifted up with sensible devotion, especially at the blessed sacrament. But when religion began to take root in my heart and I was fully convinced my soul must totally be renewed ere it could see God, I was visited with outward and inward trials.

The first thing I was called to give up for God was what the world calls my fair reputation. I had no sooner received the sacrament publicly on a weekday at St. Mary's but I was set up as a mark for all the polite students that knew me to shoot at. By this they knew that I was commenced |a| Methodist; for though there is a sacrament at the beginning of every term at which all, especially the seniors, are by statute obliged to be present, yet so dreadfully has that once faithful city played the harlot that very few masters |and| no undergraduates but the Methodists attended upon it.

Mr. Charles Wesley, whom I must always mention with the greatest deference and respect, walked with me, in order to confirm me, from the church even to the college. I confess, to my shame, I would gladly have excused him; and the next day, going to his room, one of our fellows passing by, I was ashamed to be seen to knock at his door. But, blessed be God, this fear of man gradually wore off. As I had imitated Nicodemus in his cowardice, so, by the divine assistance, I followed him in his courage. I confessed the Methodists more and more publicly every day. I walked openly with them and chose rather to bear contempt with those people of God than to enjoy the applause of almost-Christians for a season.

Soon after this, I incurred the displeasure of the master of the college, who frequently chided and once threatened to expel me if I ever visited the poor again. Being surprised at this treatment and overawed by his authority, I spoke unadvisedly with my lips and said if it displeased him, I would not. My conscience soon pricked me for this sinful compliance. I immediately repented and visited the poor |at| the first opportunity, and told my companions if ever I was called to a stake for Christ's sake, I would serve my tongue as Archbishop Cranmer served his hand, namely, make that burn first.

My tutor, being a moderate man, did not oppose me much but thought, I believe, that I went a little too far. He lent me books, gave me money, visited me, and furnished me with a physician when sick. In short, he behaved in all respects like a father; and I trust God will remember him for good, in answer to the many prayers I have put up in his behalf. . . .

Near five or six weeks I had now spent in my study, except when I was obliged to go out. During this time I was fighting with my corruptions and did little else besides kneeling down by my bedside, feeling, as it were, a heavy pressure upon my body as well as an unspeakable oppression of mind, yet offering up my soul to God to do with me as it pleased Him. It was now suggested to me that Jesus Christ was amongst the wild beasts when He was tempted and that I ought to follow his example. And being willing, as I thought, to imitate Jesus Christ, after supper I went into Christ Church Walk, near our college, and continued in silent prayer under one of the trees for near two hours, sometimes lying flat on my face, sometimes kneeling upon my knees, all the while filled with fear and concern lest some of my brethren should . . . |think me| overwhelmed with pride. The night being stormy, it gave me awful thoughts of the day of judgment. I continued, I think, till the great bell rang for retirement to the college, not without finding some reluctance in the natural man against staying so long in the cold.

The next night I repeated the same exercise at the same place. But the hour of extremity being now come, God was pleased to make an open show of those diabolical devices by which I had been deceived.

By this time, I had left off keeping my diary, using my forms or scarce my voice in prayer, visiting the prisoners, and so forth. Nothing remained for me to leave, unless I forsook public worship, but my religious friends. Now it was suggested that I must leave them also for Christ's sake. This was a sore trial; but rather than not be, as I fancied, Christ's disciple, I resolved to renounce them, though as dear to me as my own soul. Accordingly, the next day being Wednesday, whereon we kept one of our weekly fasts, instead of meeting with my brethren as usual, I went out into the fields and prayed silently by myself. Our evening meeting I neglected also and went not to breakfast, according to appointment, with Mr. Charles Wesley the day following. This, with many other concurring circumstances, made my honored friend, Mr. Charles Wesley, suspect something more than ordinary was the matter. He came to my room, soon found out my case, apprised me of my danger if I would not take advice, and recommended me to his brother John, fellow of Lincoln College, as more experienced in the spiritual life. God gave me—blessed be His holy name—a teachable temper; I waited upon his brother, with whom from that time I had the honor of growing intimate. He advised me to resume all my externals, though not to depend on them in the least. From time to time he gave me directions as my various and pitiable state required; and at length, by his excellent advice and management of me, under God, I was delivered from those wiles of Satan. Praise the Lord, O my soul, and all that is within me praise His holy name!

During this and all other seasons of temptation my soul was inwardly supported with great courage and resolution from above. Every day God made me willing to renew the combat. And though my soul, when quite empty of God, was very prone to seek satisfaction in the creature, and sometimes I fell into sensuality, yet I was generally enabled to wait in silence for the salvation of God, or to persist in prayer till some beams of spiritual light and comfort were vouchsafed me from on high. Thomas à Kempis, since translated and published by Mr. John Wesley, Castaniza's *Combat*, and the Greek Testament, every reading of which I endeavored to turn into a prayer, were of great help and furtherance to me. On receiving the holy sacrament, especially before trials, I have found grace in a very affecting manner and in abundant measure sometimes imparted to my soul—an irrefragable proof to me of the miserable delusion of the author of that work called *The Plain Account of the Sacrament*, which sinks that holy ordinance into a bare memorial; who, if he obstinately refuse the instruction of the Most High, will doubtless, without repentance, bear his punishment, whosoever he be.

To proceed—I had now taken up my externals again; and though Satan for some weeks had been biting my heel, God was pleased to show me that I should soon bruise his head. A few days after, as I was walking along I met with a poor woman whose husband was then in Bocardo, or Oxford Town jail, which I constantly visited. Seeing her much discomposed, I enquired the cause. She told me |that|, not being able to bear the crying of her children, ready to perish for hunger, and having nothing to relieve them, she had been |about| to drown herself but was mercifully prevented, and said she was coming to my room to inform me of it. I gave her some immediate relief and desired her to meet me at the prison with her husband in the afternoon. She came, and there God visited them both by His free grace. She was powerfully quickened from above; and when I had done reading, he also came to me like the trembling jailer and, grasping my hand, cried out, "I am upon the brink of hell!" From this time forward, both of them grew in grace. God, by His providence, soon delivered him from his confinement. Though notorious offenders against God and one another before, yet now they became helpmates for each other in the great work of their salvation. They are both now living and, I trust, will be my joy and crown of rejoicing in the great day of our Lord Jesus.

Soon after this the holy season of Lent came on, which our friends kept very strictly, eating no flesh during the six weeks, except on Saturdays, and also ate nothing on the other days, except on Sunday, but sage-tea without sugar and coarse bread. I constantly walked out in the cold mornings till part of one of my hands was quite black. This, with my continued abstinence and inward conflicts, at length so emaciated my body that at Passion week, finding I could scarce creep upstairs, I was obliged to inform my kind tutor of my condition, who immediately sent for a physician for me.

This caused no small triumph amongst the collegians, who began to cry out, "What is his fasting come to now?" But I rejoiced in this reproach, knowing that though I had been imprudent and lost much of my flesh, yet I had nevertheless increased in the Spirit.

This fit of sickness continued upon me for seven weeks, and a glorious visitation it was. The blessed Spirit was all this time purifying my soul. All my former gross and notorious and even my heart sins, also, were now set home upon me, of which I wrote down some remembrance immediately and confessed them before God morning and evening. Though weak, I often spent two hours in my evening retirements and prayed over my Greek Testament and Bishop Hall's most excellent *Contemplations* every hour that my health would permit.

About the end of the seven weeks, and after I had been groaning under an unspeakable pressure both of body and mind for above a twelvemonth, God was pleased to set me free in the following manner. One day, perceiving an uncommon drought and a disagreeable clamminess in my mouth and using things to allay my thirst, but in vain, it was suggested to me that when Jesus Christ cried out, "I thirst," His sufferings were near at an end. Upon which I cast myself down on the bed, crying out, "I thirst! I thirst!" Soon after this, I found and felt in myself that I was delivered from the burden that had so heavily oppressed me. The spirit of mourning was taken from me and I knew what it was truly to rejoice in God my savior and, for some time, could not avoid singing psalms wherever I was. But my joy gradually became more settled and, blessed be God, has abode and increased in my soul, saving a few casual intermissions, ever since.

Thus were the days of my mourning ended. After a long night of desertion and temptation, the star, which I had seen at a distance before, began to appear again, and the Day Star arose in my heart. Now did the Spirit of God take possession of my soul and, as I humbly hope, seal me unto the day of redemption.

WESLEY'S ALDERSGATE
EXPERIENCE

(from the *Journal* of John Wesley)

INTRODUCTION

This is one of the best-known accounts of spiritual experience in Protestant literature. It has been a continual inspiration to Anglicans as well as Methodists, particularly since the rise to prominence in nineteenth-century England and America of the Anglican evangelical movement, and the worldwide spread of Methodism in that century, especially in Canada and the United States. To this day a great host of American Episcopalians find John Wesley their spiritual father, admire greatly his refusal to part with the Church of England, and regret only his willingness to allow the American Methodists to do so.

By late April, 1738, John Wesley came to a clear understanding that the new birth was an instant experience of forgiveness, victory over sin, and assurance of salvation. He thereupon began preaching the promise of it so urgently in Anglican pulpits that weeks before he himself had found and could profess salvation by faith he was refused permission to return. In his account of the crucial prayer meeting on Aldersgate Street, Wesley tells us that the reading of Luther's preface to his commentary on the Epistle to the Romans greatly affected him. Wesley apparently had not read Luther carefully, and did not notice the failure of the great reformer to emphasize a transformed life. When he discovered that omission two years later, while reading Luther's preface to his commentary on Galatians, Wesley denounced it both privately and publicly. But Luther's emphasis upon salvation by grace fit precisely the needs of the leader of the Holy Club; for he had long trusted, perhaps only half-consciously, in salvation by his own good works.

However, the lines so often quoted from this testimony ("I felt my heart strangely warmed. I felt I did trust in Christ, and Christ alone, for salvation") not only truncate Wesley's account but circumscribe his doctrine. The next words, rarely quoted, were equally important: "An assurance was given me that He had taken away *my* sins, even *mine*, and saved *me* from the law of sin and death." This moral fruit of conversion was for Wesley, then and thereafter, the witness of his own spirit, as he put it in a later sermon, to the fact of his salvation. The *Journal* finds him again and again coming back to that pivotal element in assurance, deliverance from the dominion of sin.

One final note is to remember the circumstances of the publication of this first segment of Wesley's *Journal*. He kept a diary, often cryptic and sometimes in code, for his own personal edification. His *Journal*, however, was written for publication, and must be construed as a part of his effort to expound Christian doctrine.

This portion of the *Journal*, in fact, was prepared for publication over two years later and printed in 1740. By that time, Wesley was locked in controversy with the London Moravians, who put the doctrine of the new birth so high that few could testify to having achieved it. On that account, the Moravians sensed no need of a "second experience" of purity of heart and perfect love. Wesley, however, became convinced in the fall of 1739 that many of the biblical promises referred not only to the new birth but to a further experience of entire sanctification. One must consider this volume of the *Journal*, therefore, and particularly that portion of it describing this trip to two Moravian centers in Germany, immediately after Aldersgate, to be a chapter in his long war of words with the London Moravians. Here, then, is proof that people who sincerely believed in the new birth might differ upon its details, even though they agreed that it brought deliverance from sin and assurance of salvation.

❖ ❖ ❖

Friday, 19 [*May*, 1738]. My brother had a second return of his pleurisy. A few of us spent Saturday night in prayer. The next day, being Whitsunday—after hearing Dr. Heylin preach a truly Christian sermon (on "They were all filled with the Holy Ghost." "And so," said he, "may all you be, if it is not your own fault") and assisting him at the Holy Communion (his curate being taken ill in the church)—I received the surprising news that my brother had found rest to his soul. His bodily strength returned also from that hour. "Who is so great a God as our God?"

I preached at St. John's, Wapping, at three, and at St.

Benet's, Paul's Wharf, in the evening. At these churches, likewise, I am to preach no more. At St. Antholin's I preached for the last time on the Thursday following.

Monday, *Tuesday*, and *Wednesday* I had continual sorrow and heaviness in my heart, something of which I described in the broken manner I was able in the following letter to a friend:

> Oh, why is it that so great, so wise, so holy a God will use such an instrument as me! Lord, "let the dead bury their dead"! But will you send the dead to raise the dead? Yea, you send whom you *will send*, and show mercy by whom you *will* show mercy! Amen! Be it then according to your will! If you speak the word, Judas shall cast out devils.
>
> I feel what you say (though not enough), for I am under the same condemnation. I see that the whole law of God is holy and just and good. I know every thought, every temper of my soul, ought to bear God's image and superscription. But how am I fallen from the glory of God! I feel that "I am sold under sin." I know that I too deserve nothing but wrath, being full of all abominations and having no good thing in me to atone for them, or to remove the wrath of God. All my works, my righteousness, my prayers need an atonement for themselves; so that my mouth is stopped. I have nothing to plead. God is holy; I am unholy. God is a consuming fire; I am altogether a sinner, meet to be consumed.
>
> Yet I hear a voice (and is it not the voice of God?) saying, "Believe and thou shalt be saved. He that believeth is passed from death unto life. God so loved the world that He gave His only begotten Son, that whosoever believeth in Him should not perish but have everlasting life."
>
> O, let no one deceive us by vain words, as if we had already attained this faith! By its fruits we shall know. Do we already feel "peace with God" and "joy in the Holy Ghost?" Does His "Spirit bear witness with our spirit that we are the children of God"? Alas! with mine He does not. Nor, I fear, with yours. O Savior of men, save us from trusting in anything but *you*! Draw us after you! Let us be emptied of ourselves, and then fill us with peace and joy in believing, and let nothing separate us from your love in time or in eternity.

What occurred on *Wednesday* 24th, I think best to relate at large, after premising what may make it the better understood.

Let him that cannot receive it ask of the Father of lights that He would give more light both to him and me.

1. I believe, till I was about ten years old, I had not sinned away that "washing of the Holy Ghost" which was given me in baptism, having been strictly educated and carefully taught that I could only be saved "by universal obedience, by keeping all the commandments of God"—in the meaning of which I was diligently instructed. And those instructions, so far as they respected outward duties and sins, I gladly received and often thought of. But all that was said to me of inward obedience or holiness I neither understood nor remembered. So that I was indeed as ignorant of the true meaning of the law as I was of the gospel of Christ.

2. The next six or seven years were spent at school, where, outward restraints being removed, I was much more negligent than before, even of outward duties, and almost continually guilty of outward sins which I knew to be such, though they were not scandalous in the eye of the world. However, I still read the Scriptures and said my prayers, morning and evening. And what I now hoped to be saved by was (1) "not being so bad as other people"; (2) having still a kindness for religion; and (3) "reading the Bible, and going to church, and saying my prayers."

3. Being removed to the university for five years, I still said my prayers both in public and in private and read with the Scriptures several other books of religion, especially comments on the New Testament. Yet I had not all the while so much as a notion of inward holiness, nay, went on habitually, and (for the most part) very contentedly, in some or other known sin— indeed, with some intermissions and short struggles, especially before and after the Holy Communion, which I was obliged to receive thrice a year. I cannot well tell what I hoped to be saved by now, when I was continually sinning against that little light I had, unless by those transient fits of what many divines taught me to call "repentance."

4. When I was about twenty-two, my father pressed me to enter into Holy Orders. At the same time, the providence of God directing me to [Thomas à] Kempis's *Christian Pattern*, I began to see that true religion was seated in the heart and that God's law extended to all our thoughts as well as words and actions. I was, however, very angry at Kempis for being *too strict*, though I read him only in Dean Stanhope's translation. Yet I had frequently much sensible comfort in reading him, such as I was an utter stranger to before. And meeting likewise with a religious friend, which I had never had till now, I began to alter the whole form of my conversation and to set in earnest upon "a new life." I set apart an hour or two a day for religious retirement. I communicated every week. I watched against all sins, whether in word or deed. I began to aim at, and pray for, inward holiness. So that now, "doing so much and living so good a life," I doubted not but I was a good Christian.

5. Removing soon after to another college, I executed a resolution which I was before convinced was of the utmost importance—shaking off at once all my trifling acquaintance. I began to see more and more the value of time. I applied myself closer to study. I watched more carefully against actual sins. I advised others to be religious, according to that scheme of religion by which I modeled my own life. But meeting now with Mr. [William] Law's *Christian Perfection* and *Serious Call*, (although I was much offended at many parts of both, yet) they convinced me more than ever of the exceeding height and breadth and depth of the law of God. The light flowed in so mightily upon my soul that everything appeared in a new view. I cried to God for help and resolved not to prolong the time of obeying Him, as I had never done before. And by my continued "endeavor to keep His whole law," inward and outward, "to the utmost of my power," I was persuaded that I should be accepted of Him and that I was even then in a state of salvation.

6. In 1730 I began visiting the prisons, assisting the poor and sick in town, and doing what other good I could by my presence or my little fortune to the bodies and souls of all men. To this end I abridged myself of all superfluities, and many that are called necessaries of life. I soon became a "by-word" for so doing, and I rejoiced that "my name was cast out as evil." The next spring I began observing the Wednesday and Friday fasts commonly observed in the ancient Church, tasting no food till three in the afternoon. And now I knew not how to go any further. I diligently strove against all sin. I omitted no sort of self-denial which I thought lawful. I carefully used, both in public and in private, all the means of grace at all opportunities. I omitted no occasion of doing good. I for that reason suffered evil. And all this I knew to be nothing unless as it was directed toward inward holiness. Accordingly this, the image of God, was what I aimed at in all, by doing His will, not my own. Yet when, after continuing some years in this course, I apprehended myself to be near death, I could not find that all this gave me any comfort nor any assurance of acceptance with God. At this I was then not a little surprised, not imagining I had been all this time building on the sand, nor considering that "other foundation can no man lay than that which is laid by God, even Christ Jesus."

7. Soon after, a contemplative man convinced me still more than I was convinced before that outward works are nothing, being alone, and in several conversations instructed me how to pursue inward holiness, or a union of the soul with God. But even of his instructions (though I then received them as the words of God) I cannot but now observe (1) that he spoke so incautiously against *trusting* in *outward works* that he discouraged me from *doing* them at all; (2) that he recommended (as it were, to supply what was wanting in them) *mental prayer* and the like exercises, as the most effectual means of purifying the soul and uniting it with God. Now these were, in truth, as much *my own works* as visiting the sick or clothing the naked; and the "union with God" thus pursued was as really "my own righteousness" as any I had before pursued under another name.

8. In this *refined* way of trusting to my own works and my own righteousness (so zealously inculcated by the *mystic* writers, whom I declare, in my cool judgment and in the presence of the most high God, I believe to be one great antichrist), I dragged on heavily, finding no comfort or help therein till the time of my leaving England. On shipboard, however, I was again active in outward works, where it pleased God of his free mercy to give me twenty-six of the Moravian brethren for companions, who endeavored to show me a more excellent way. But I understood it not at first. I was too learned and too wise, so that it seemed foolishness unto me. And I continued preaching and following after, and trusting in that righteousness whereby no flesh can be justified.

9. All the time I was at Savannah I was thus "beating the air." Being ignorant of the righteousness of Christ which, by a

living faith in him, bringeth salvation "to every one that
believeth," I sought to establish my own righteousness, and so
labored in the fire all my days. I was now properly "under the
law." I knew that "the law" of God was "spiritual; I consented to it
that it was good." Yea, "I delighted in it after the inner man." Yet
was I "carnal, sold under sin." Every day was I constrained to cry
out, "What I do, I allow not; for what I would, I do not, but what I
hate, that I do. To will is indeed present with me; but how to
perform that which is good, I find not. For the good which I would,
I do not, but the evil which I would not, that I do. I find a law that
when I would do good, evil is present" with me, even the "law in
my members, warring against the law of my mind" and still
"bringing me into captivity to the law of sin."

10. In this vile, abject state of bondage to sin I was indeed
fighting continually, but not conquering. Before, I had willingly
served sin; now it was unwillingly, but still I served it. I fell and
rose and fell again. Sometimes I was overcome and in heaviness;
sometimes I overcame and was in joy. For as in the former state I
had some foretastes of the terrors of the law, so had I in this of
the comforts of the gospel. During this whole struggle between
nature and grace (which had now continued above ten years), I
had many remarkable returns to prayer, especially when I was in
trouble. I had many sensible comforts, which are indeed no other
than short anticipations of the life of faith. But I was still "under
the law," not "under grace" (the state most who are called
Christians are content to live and die in), for I was only "striving
with," not "freed from, sin." Neither had I "the witness of the
Spirit with my spirit," and indeed could not, for I "sought it not by
faith, (but as it were) by the works of the law."

11. In my return to England, January 1738, being in
imminent danger of death and very uneasy on that account, I was
strongly convinced that the cause of that uneasiness was unbelief
and that the gaining a true, living faith was the "one thing
needful" for me. But still I fixed not this faith on its right object: I
meant only faith in God, not faith in or through Christ. Again, I
knew not that I was *wholly void of this faith* but only thought I *had not
enough of it.* So that when Peter Böhler, whom God prepared for
me as soon as I came to London, affirmed of true faith in Christ
(which is but one) that it had those two fruits inseparably

attending it, "dominion over sin, and constant peace from a sense of forgiveness," I was quite amazed and looked upon it as a new gospel. If this was so, it was clear I had not faith. But I was not willing to be convinced of this. Therefore I disputed with all my might and labored to prove that faith might be where these were not, especially where that sense of forgiveness was not; for all the Scriptures relating to this I had been long since taught to construe away and to call all "Presbyterians" who spoke otherwise. Besides, I well saw no one could, in the nature of things, have such a sense of forgiveness and not *feel* it. But I felt it not. If, then, there was no faith without this, all my pretensions to faith dropped at once.

12. When I met Peter Böhler again, he readily consented to put the dispute upon the issue which I desired, namely, Scripture and experience. I first consulted the Scripture. But when I set aside the glosses of men and simply considered the words of God, comparing them together and endeavoring to illustrate the obscure by the plainer passages, I found they all made against me and was forced to retreat to my last hold, "that experience would never agree with the *literal interpretation* of those Scriptures. Nor could I therefore allow it to be the truth, till I found some living witnesses of it." He replied he "could show me such at any time—if I desired it, the next day." And accordingly, the next day he came again with three others, all of whom testified of their own personal experience that a true living faith in Christ is inseparable from a sense of pardon for all past, and freedom from all present sins. They added with one mouth that this faith was the gift, the free gift of God, and that He would surely bestow it upon every soul who earnestly and perseveringly sought it. I was now thoroughly convinced and, by the grace of God, I resolved to seek it unto the end, (1) by absolutely renouncing all dependence, in whole or in part, upon *my own* works or righteousness—on which I had really grounded my hope of salvation, though I knew it not, from my youth up; (2) by adding to "the constant use of all the" other "means of grace" continual prayer for this very thing— justifying, saving faith, a full reliance on the blood of Christ shed for *me*, a trust in Him, as *my Christ*, as my sole justification, sanctification, and redemption.

13. I continued thus to seek it (though with strange

indifference, dullness, and coldness, and unusually frequent relapses into sin) till *Wednesday*, May 24. I think it was about five this morning, that I opened my Testament on those words. . .* "There are given unto us exceeding great and precious promises, even that you should be partakers of the divine nature" (2 Peter 1:4). Just as I went out, I opened it again on those words, "You are not far from the kingdom of God." In the afternoon I was asked to go to St. Paul's [Cathedral]. The anthem was

> Out of the deep have I called unto thee, O Lord. Lord, hear my voice. O let thine ears consider well the voice of my complaint. If thou, Lord, wilt be extreme to mark what is done amiss, O Lord, who may abide it? But there is mercy with Thee; therefore shalt thou be feared. O Israel, trust in the Lord, for with the Lord there is mercy and with Him is plenteous redemption. And He shall redeem Israel from all his sins.

14. In the evening, I went very unwillingly to a society in Aldersgate Street, where one was reading Luther's preface to the Epistle to the Romans. About a quarter before nine, while he was describing the change which God works in the heart through faith in Christ, I felt my heart strangely warmed. I felt I did trust in Christ, Christ alone for salvation; and an assurance was given me that He had taken away *my* sins, even *mine*, and saved *me* from the law of sin and death.

15. I began to pray with all my might for those who had in a more especial manner despitefully used me and persecuted me. I then testified openly to all there what I now first felt in my heart. But it was not long before the enemy suggested, "This cannot be faith, for where is your joy?" Then was I taught that peace and victory over sin are essential to faith in the Captain of our salvation but that, as to the transports of joy that usually attend the beginning of it, especially in those who have mourned deeply, "God sometimes gives, sometimes withholds them, according to the counsels of His will."

16. After my return home, I was much buffeted with temptations, but cried out and they fled away. They returned

---

*Wesley's quotation of the Greek text is omitted.

again and again. I as often lifted up my eyes and He "sent me help from His holy place." And herein I found [where] the difference between this and my former state chiefly consisted. I was striving, yea, fighting with all my might under the law, as well as under grace. But then I was sometimes, if not often, conquered; now, I was always conqueror.

Thur., May 25. The moment I awaked, "Jesus, Master," was in my heart and in my mouth, and I found all my strength lay in keeping my eye fixed upon Him and my soul waiting on Him continually. Being again at St. Paul's in the afternoon, I could taste the good Word of God in the anthem, which began, "My song shall be always of the loving-kindness of the Lord: with my mouth will I ever be showing forth thy truth from one generation to another." Yet the enemy injected a fear, "If you do believe, why is there not a more sensible change?" I answered (yet not I): "That I know not. But this I know, I have *now peace with God. And I sin not today*, and Jesus my Master has forbid me to take thought for the morrow."

"But is not *any* sort of *fear* (continued the tempter) a proof that you do not believe?" I desired my Master to answer for me, and opened His book upon those words of St. Paul, "Without were fightings, within were fears." Then, inferred I, well may fears be within *me*, but I must go on and tread them under my feet.

Fri., May 26. My soul continued in peace, but yet in heaviness because of manifold temptations. I asked Mr. Töltschig, the Moravian, what to do. He said, "You must not fight with them as you did before, but flee from them the moment they appear and take shelter in the wounds of Jesus." The same I learned also from the afternoon anthem, which was, "My soul truly waiteth still upon God for of Him cometh my salvation; He verily is my strength and my salvation, He is my defense, so that I shall not greatly fall. O put your trust in Him alway, ye people; pour out your hearts before Him, for God is our hope."

Sat. 27. Believing one reason of my want of joy was want of time for prayer, I resolved to do no business till I went to church in the morning, but continued pouring out my heart before Him. And this day my spirit was enlarged so that, though I was now also assaulted by many temptations, I was more than conqueror, gaining more power thereby to trust and to rejoice in God my Savior.

Sun. 28. I waked in peace but not in joy. In the same even, quiet state I was till the evening, when I was roughly attacked in a large company as an enthusiast, a seducer, and a setter-forth of new doctrines. By the blessing of God I was not moved to anger, but after a calm and short reply went away, though not with so tender a concern as was due to those who were seeking death in the error of their life.

This day I preached in the morning at St. George's, Bloomsbury, on "This is the victory that overcometh the world, even our faith" and in the afternoon at the chapel in Long Acre on God's justifying the ungodly—the last time (I understand) I am to preach at either. "Not as I will, but as You will."

Mon. 29. I set out for Dummer with Mr. Wolf, one of the first-fruits of Peter Böhler's ministry in England. I was much strengthened by the grace of God in him; yet was his state so far above mine that I was often tempted to doubt whether we had one faith. But without much reasoning about it, I held here: "Though his be *strong* and mine *weak*, yet that God has given *some degree* of faith even to me, I know by its fruits. For I have *constant peace*, not one uneasy thought. And I have *freedom from sin*, not one unholy desire."

Yet on Wednesday did I grieve the Spirit of God not only by not "watching unto prayer" but likewise by speaking with sharpness instead of tender love of one that was not sound in the faith. Immediately God hid His face and I was troubled, and in this heaviness I continued till the next morning, June 1, when it pleased God, while I was exhorting another, to give comfort to *my* soul and, after I had spent some time in prayer, to direct me to those gracious words, "Having therefore boldness to enter into the holiest by the blood of Jesus, let us draw near with a true heart in full assurance of faith. Let us hold fast the profession of our faith without wavering (for He is faithful that promised), and let us consider one another to provoke unto love and to good works."

Saturday, June 3. I was so strongly assaulted by one of my old enemies that I had scarce strength to open my lips or even to look up for help. But after I had prayed faintly as I could, the temptation vanished away.

Sun. 4. Was indeed a feast day. For from the time of my

rising till past one in the afternoon, I was praying, reading the Scriptures, singing praise, or calling sinners to repentance. All these days I scarce remember to have opened the Testament but upon some great and precious promise. And I saw more than ever that the gospel is in truth but one great promise from the beginning of it to the end.

Tues. 6. I had still more comfort and peace and joy, on which, I fear, I began to presume. For in the evening I received a letter from Oxford which threw me into much perplexity. It was asserted therein "that no doubting could consist with the least degree of true faith; that whoever at any time felt any doubt or fear was not 'weak in the faith' but had *no faith* at all; and that none hath any faith till the law of the Spirit of life has made him *wholly* free from the law of sin and death."

Begging of God to direct me, I opened my Testament on I Corinthians 3:1 and following, where St. Paul speaks of those whom he terms "babes in Christ," who were "not able to bear strong meat," nay (in a sense), "carnal"; to whom nevertheless he says, "You are God's building, you are the temple of God." Surely, then, these men had *some degree* of faith, though, it is plain, their faith was but *weak*.

After some hours spent in the Scripture and prayer, I was much comforted. Yet I felt a kind of soreness in my heart, so that I found my wound was not fully healed. O God, save me, and all that are "weak in the faith," from "doubtful disputation."

Wed. June 7. I determined, if God should permit, to retire for a short time into Germany. I had fully proposed before I left Georgia so to do, if it should please God to bring me back to Europe. And I now clearly saw the time was come. My weak mind could not bear to be thus sawn asunder. And I hoped the conversing with those holy men who were themselves living witnesses of the full power of faith, and yet able to bear with those that are weak, would be a means, under God, of so establishing my soul that I might "go on from faith to faith and from strength to strength."

THE NATURE AND NECESSITY OF OUR REGENERATION OR NEW BIRTH IN CHRIST JESUS

by George Whitefield

INTRODUCTION

This is George Whitefield's earliest published work and is one of the most influential sermons ever published in Christendom. Not only did it spark the evangelical awakening in England, turning the Holy Club outward toward the largely unchurched masses, but it helped spread a revival movement in America that has often been called "The Great Awakening." Whitefield first printed the sermon in London in 1737, while John and Charles Wesley were still bogged down in their mission to Georgia; it became a sensation, and was reprinted at once in Philadelphia and Boston. After reading it the Boston clergy almost unanimously invited Whitefield to bring the awakening to their congregations. He arrived in September, 1740, was escorted into the city by nearly all the ministers of the town, and preached in almost all their pulpits.

The popular view, still being repeated by responsible historians, that on his own initiative Whitefield brought enthusiastic evangelicalism to that staid city will not hold water. His preaching in fact sustained Puritan doctrines of the new birth that were by then over a century old, and on nearly every pastor's lips. When he left three weeks later, the same ministers escorted him as far as Worcester. He spent two and one-half days in Northampton visiting with Jonathan Edwards. Edwards added nothing whatever to his views, but his wife made a great impression upon the young evangelist.

The substance of this discourse belies the charge of enthusiasm so often placed against George Whitefield. Though he always agreed that facing the truth about life and death and eternal salvation deeply stirred the emotions of thinking men and women, he anchored the doctrine of the new birth in the New Testament, as had the great Anglican, William

Law, in his book on *Christian Perfection*, published a decade before. Law had emphasized being made a "new creature" through the promised gift of the Holy Spirit, as St. Paul had, and stressed the purity of heart and perfection of moral conduct which Jesus and Paul had said were the believer's privilege. Whitefield read Law's volume after the Wesleys led him into the Holy Club in 1734 or 1735. In fact, Law, Whitefield, and the Wesleys did not add anything new to what Puritans everywhere had preached about righteous conduct, save for their stress upon the biblical term perfection. John and Charles Wesleys' grandparents had been Puritans. Though their parents had returned to the Anglican Church, they trained their children in Puritan morality and piety.

Historians, alas, have paid too much attention to the response to Whitefield's preaching and not enough to the content of his sermons. Wesley could scarcely have developed such admiration for him if there had been any doubt about the thoroughness of Whitefield's understanding of the biblical promises of a present experience of salvation. What Wesley says he learned from the Moravians, namely, that regeneration was instantaneous and brought both conscious assurance of forgiveness and deliverance from sin, Whitefield seems to have gotten from William Law and from his association with the Holy Club. That fact raises questions as to how much Peter Böhler and the Moravians actually taught Wesley, as distinct from what they led him to appropriate for himself.

A summary of these doctrines can be found in the sermon. However, a few comments about its pentecostal language are appropriate. Whitefield proclaimed the sanctification of our "corrupt natures" and the promise of being renewed in the image of God, just as the New Testament does, but said those things take place in regeneration. He also declared that Paul's preaching on the Holy Spirit to the Ephesians, and the outpouring of the Spirit on that group, was an example of the new birth. He thus used the phrase "baptism with the Holy Ghost" to denote regeneration. Wesley did this occasionally in his *Journal* and correspondence, but only before autumn 1739. After that, the two Wesleys rarely used that language and then only to refer to a second moment of grace, which they called variously purity of heart, perfect love, full salvation, entire sanctification, or full restoration in the divine image.

All of their earlier uses of the phrase, "baptism with the Holy Spirit," were geared to the assumption, which at the outset Law, the Wesleys, and Whitefield shared, that the New Testament taught only one moment of saving grace, but that it was a more sublime experience than we ordinarily think and marked the beginning of a holy life. After Wesley became convinced that some of this scriptural language referred to a second and deeper experience of sanctification, he reserved the terms full salvation, holiness of heart, and Christian perfection for that second experience. He stopped using "baptism with the Holy Ghost" altogether, but declared that heart purity came when believers were "filled with the Holy Spirit" or "filled with pure love." The reason for this, I have argued elsewhere,* was not only Wesley's desire to limit his teaching to words which he believed Scripture used to mean exactly what he was using them to mean, but his eagerness not to contradict Whitefield merely on terminology.

It is evident that Whitefield's preaching of such a radical transformation must have affected not only unchurched people in England and America, but those on both sides of the ocean who regarded themselves as Christians. If his hearers did not claim to have experienced a dramatic change from the old life to that of a "new creature" in Christ, he told them, they had not been born again. Whitefield convinced many thousands to seek and find and testify to that experience, with what both the evangelist and his converts later discovered was too much abandon.

Wesley was making that discovery in England in the fall of 1739, as his young friend sailed back to America. It had special poignancy because of the Moravian insistence that those who had not seen all doubt and fear vanish were not regenerate at all. Neither Whitefield nor the Wesleys could believe this, and pointed to the occasions when biblical saints, and their own converts, knew fear and doubt.

❖   ❖   ❖

"If any man be in Christ, he is a new creature" (2 Cor. 5:17).

The doctrine of our regeneration, or new birth in Christ Jesus, though one of the most fundamental doctrines of our holy religion; though so plainly and often pressed on us in sacred writ "that he that runs may read"; nay, though it is the very hinge on which the salvation of each of us turns, and a point too in which all sincere Christians, of whatever denomination, agree; yet is so seldom considered and so little experimentally understood by the generality of professors that, were we to judge of the truth of it by the experience of most who call themselves Christians, we should be apt to imagine they had "not so much as heard" whether there be any such thing as regeneration or no.

---

*"John Wesley and the Second Blessing," forthcoming in the *Wesleyan Theological Journal* 21 (Spring, 1986).

It is true, men, for the most part, are orthodox in the common articles of their creed. They believe there is but one God and one mediator between God and man, even the man Christ Jesus, and that there is no other name given under heaven whereby they can be saved, besides His. But then tell them they must be regenerate, they must be born again, they must be renewed in the very spirit, that is, in the inmost faculties of their minds, ere they can truly call Christ Lord, Lord, or have any share in the merits of His precious blood, and they are ready to cry out with Nicodemus, "How can these things be?" Or with the Athenians, on another occasion, "What will this babbler say? He seemeth to be a setter-forth of strange doctrines, because we preach unto them Christ, and the new birth."

That I may therefore contribute my mite towards curing the fatal mistake of such persons, who would thus put asunder what God has inseparably joined together, and vainly expect to be justified by Christ, that is, have their sins forgiven, unless they are also sanctified, that is, have their nature changed and made holy, I shall beg leave to enlarge on the words of the text in the following manner:

First, I shall endeavor to explain what is meant by being in Christ: "if any man be in Christ."

Secondly, what we are to understand by being a new creature: "if any man be in Christ," says the apostle, "he is a new creature."

Thirdly, I shall produce some arguments to prove why we must be new creatures ere we can be "in Christ."

Fourthly and lastly, I shall draw some inferences from what will have been delivered, and then conclude with a word or two of exhortation from the whole.

And *first* then, I am to endeavor to explain what is meant by this expression in the text, "If any man be in Christ."

Now a person may be said to be in Christ two ways. First, only by an outward profession. And in this sense, every one that is called a Christian or baptized into Christ's church may be said to be in Christ. But that this is not the sole meaning of the apostle's phrase now before us is evident, because then "everyone that names the name of Christ" or is baptized into His invisible church would be a new creature. Which is notoriously false, it being too plain, beyond all contradiction, that comparatively but few of those that are "born of water" are "born of the Spirit" likewise; or, to use another scriptural way of speaking, many are baptized with water which were never, effectually at least, baptized with the Holy Ghost.

To be in Christ therefore, in the full import of the word, must certainly mean something more than a bare outward profession or being called after His name. For as this same apostle tells us, "all are not Israelites that are of Israel," that is, when applied to Christianity, all are not *real* Christians that are nominally such. Nay, this is so far from being the case that our blessed Lord Himself informs us that many that have prophesied or preached in His name, and in His name cast out devils and done many wonderful works, shall notwithstanding be dismissed at the last day with a "depart from me, I know you not, you workers of iniquity."

It remains, therefore, that this expression, "If any man be in Christ," must be understood in a second and closer signification, namely, to be in Him so as to partake of the benefits of His sufferings; to be in Him not only by an outward profession but by an inward change and purity of heart and cohabitation of His Holy Spirit; to be in Him so as to be mystically united to Him by a true and lively faith, and thereby to receive spiritual virtue from Him, as the members of the natural body do from the head, or the branches from the vine; to be in Him in such a manner as the apostle, speaking of himself, acquaints us he knew a person was: "I knew a man in Christ," says he, that is, a true Christian. Or, as he himself desires to be in Christ when he wishes, in his Epistle to the Philippians, that he might be found "in Him."

This is undoubtedly the full purport of the apostle's expressions in the words of the text. So that what he says in his Epistle to the Romans about circumcision may very well be applied to the present subject, namely, that he is not a real Christian who is only one outwardly, nor is that true baptism which is only outward in the flesh. But he is a true Christian who is one inwardly, whose baptism is that of the heart, in the Spirit, and not merely in the water; whose praise is not of man but of God.

Or, as he speaketh in another place, neither circumcision nor uncircumcision availeth any thing of itself, but a new creature. Which amounts to what he here declares in the verse now under consideration, that if any man be truly and properly in Christ, he is a new creature.

What we are to understand by being a "new creature" was the next and *second* general thing to be considered.

And here it is evident at the first view that this expression is not to be so explained as though there was a physical change required to be made in us, that is, as though we were to be reduced to our primitive nothings and then created and formed again. For supposing we were, as Nicodemus ignorantly imagined, to enter a "second time into our mother's womb, and be born," alas, what would it contribute towards rendering us spiritually "new creatures"? Since that which was born of flesh would be flesh still, we should be the same carnal persons as ever, being derived from carnal parents, and consequently receiving the seeds of all manner of sin and corruption from them.

No, it only means that we must be so altered as to the qualities and tempers of our minds that we must entirely forget what manner of persons we once were. As it may be said of a piece of gold that was in the ore, after it has been cleansed, purified, and polished, that it is a new piece of gold; as it may be said of a bright glass that has been covered over with filth, when it is wiped and so become transparent and clear, that it is a new glass; or as it might be said of Naaman, when he recovered of his leprosy and his flesh returned unto him again like the flesh of a young child, that he was a new man—so our souls, though still the same as to essence, yet are so purged, purified, and cleansed from their natural dross, filth, and leprosy by the blessed influences of the Holy Spirit, that they may properly be said to be made anew.

How this glorious change is wrought in the soul cannot easily be explained. For no one knows the ways of the Spirit, save the Spirit of God Himself. Not that this ought to be any argument against this doctrine. For as our blessed Lord observed to Nicodemus when he was discoursing on this very subject, "The wind," says He, "blows where it lists, and you hear the sound thereof, but cannot tell whence it comes and whither it goes." And if we are told of natural things and we understand them not, how much less ought we to wonder if we cannot immediately account for the invisible workings of the Holy Spirit? The truth of the matter is this: the doctrine of our regeneration or new birth in Christ Jesus is "dark and hard to be understood" by the natural man.

But that there is really such a thing and that each of us must be spiritually born again before we can enter into the kingdom of God or, to keep to the terms made use of in the text, must be "new creatures" before we can be "in Christ," I shall endeavor to show under my *third* general head; in which I was to produce some arguments to prove why we must be new creatures in order to qualify us for being savingly in Christ.

And here one would think it sufficient to affirm that God himself, in His Holy Word, has told us so. For not to mention many texts that might be produced out of the Old Testament to prove this point (and indeed, by the way, one would wonder how Nicodemus, who was a teacher in Israel and who was therefore to instruct the people in the spiritual meaning of the law, should be so ignorant of this grand article as we find he really was, by his asking our blessed Lord, when he was pressing on Him this topic, "How can these things be?" Surely, he could not forget how often the Psalmist had begged of God to make him a new heart and renew a right spirit within him, and likewise how frequently the prophets had warned the people to make them new hearts and new minds and so turn unto the Lord their God.) But not to mention these and such like texts out of the Old Testament, this doctrine is so plainly and often repeated in the New that, as I observed before, "he that runs may read." For what says the great prophet and instructor of the world Himself? "Except a man (that is, every one that is naturally engendered of the offspring of Adam) be born again of water and of the Spirit, he cannot enter into the kingdom of God." And lest we should be apt to slight this assertion and, Nicodemus-like, reject the doctrine because we cannot immediately explain how this thing can be, our blessed Master therefore affirms it, as it were, by an oath, "Verily, verily, I say unto you" (or, as it may be read, I the amen, I, who am truth itself, say unto you that it is the unalterable appointment of my heavenly Father) "that unless a man be born again, he cannot enter the kingdom of God."

Agreeable to this are those many passages we meet within the epistles where we are commanded to be renewed in the Spirit, that is, as was before explained, in the inmost faculties of our minds; to put off the old man, which is corrupt, and to put on the "new man," which is created after God, in righteousness and true holiness; that "old things" must pass away and that all things must become new; that we are to be saved by the washing of regeneration and the renewing of the Holy Ghost. Or, methinks, was there no other passage to be produced besides the words of the text, it would be full enough, since the apostle therein positively affirms that "if any man be in Christ, he is a new creature."

Now what can be understood by all these different terms of being born again, of putting off the old man and putting on the new, of being renewed in the spirit of our minds and becoming new creatures, but that Christianity requires a thorough, real, inward change of heart? Do we think these and such like forms of speaking are mere metaphors, words of a bare sound, without any real solid signification? Indeed, it is to be feared some men would have them interpreted so. But alas, unhappy men, they are not to be envied their metaphorical interpretation. It will be well if they do not interpret themselves out of their salvation.

Multitudes of other texts might be produced to confirm this same truth. But those already quoted are so plain and convincing that one would imagine no one should deny it, were we not told there are some who, having eyes, see not, and ears, hear not, and that will not understand with their hearts or hear with their ears, lest they should be converted and Christ should heal them.

But I proceed to a second argument to prove why we must be new creatures, in order to be rightly in Christ. And that shall be taken from the purity of God and the present corrupt and polluted state of man.

Now God is described in Holy Scripture (and I speak to those who profess to know the Scripture) as a spirit, as a being of such infinite sanctity as to be of purer eyes than to behold iniquity, as to be so transcendently holy that it is said the very heavens are not clean in His sight. And the angels themselves He chargeth with folly. On the other hand, man is described (and every regenerate person will find it true by his own experience) as a creature altogether conceived and born in sin, as having no good thing dwelling in him, as being "carnal, sold under sin," nay, as having a mind which is "enmity with God," and such like. And since, then, there is such an infinite disparity, can any one conceive how such a filthy, corrupted, polluted wretch can dwell with an infinitely pure and holy God before he is changed, and rendered in some measure like Him? Can He that is of purer eyes than to behold iniquity dwell with it? Can He in whose sight the heavens are not clean delight to dwell with uncleanness itself? No; we might as well suppose light to have communion with darkness, or Christ to have concord with Belial.

But I pass on to a third argument to make good the apostle's assertion in the text, which shall be founded on the consideration of the nature of that happiness God has prepared for those that unfeignedly love Him.

To enter indeed on a minute and particular description of heaven would be vain and presumptuous, since we are told that eye hath not seen, nor ear heard, neither hath it entered into the heart of man to conceive the things that are there prepared for the sincere followers of the holy Jesus. However, this we may venture to affirm in general, that as God is a spirit, so the happiness He has laid up for His people is spiritual likewise; and consequently, unless our carnal minds are changed and become spiritualized, we can never be made meet to partake of that inheritance with the saints in light.

It is true we may flatter ourselves that, supposing we continue in our natural corrupt estate and carry all our lusts along with us, we should, notwithstanding, relish heaven, was God to admit us therein. And so we might, was it a Mohammedan paradise wherein we were to take our full swing in sensual delights. But since its joys are only spiritual and no unclean thing can possibly enter those blessed mansions, there is an absolute necessity of our being changed and undergoing a total renovation of our depraved natures, before we can have any taste or relish of those heavenly pleasures.

It is doubtless for this reason that the apostle declares it to be the irrevocable decree of the Almighty that without holiness, that is, without being made pure by regeneration and having the image of God thereby reinstamped upon the soul, no man living shall see the Lord. And it is very observable that our divine Master, in the famous passage before referred to concerning the absolute necessity of regeneration, does not say, unless a man be born again he *shall not*, but unless a man be born again he *cannot* enter into the kingdom of God. For it is founded in the very nature of things that unless we have dispositions wrought in us suitable and answerable to the objects that are to entertain us, we can take no manner of complacency or satisfaction in them. For instance, what delight can the most harmonious music afford a deaf, or what pleasure can the most excellent picture give a blind man? Can a tasteless palate relish the richest dainties, or a filthy swine be pleased with the finest garden of flowers? No. And what reason can be assigned for it? An answer is ready: because they have neither of them any tempers of mind correspondent or agreeable to what they are to be diverted with. And thus it is with the soul hereafter. For death makes no more alteration in the soul than as it enlarges its faculties and makes it capable of receiving deeper impressions either of pleasure or pain. If it delighted to converse with God here, it will be transported with the sight of His glorious majesty hereafter. If it was pleased with the communion of saints on earth, it will be infinitely more so with the communion and society of holy angels and the spirits of just men made perfect in heaven. But if the opposite of all this be true, we may assure ourselves it could not be happy, was God himself to admit it (which He never will do) into the regions of the blessed.

But it is time for me to hasten to the *fourth* and last argument I shall offer to prove that we must be new creatures, ere we can be in Christ, namely, because Christ's redemption will not be complete without it.

If we reflect indeed on the first and chief end of our blessed Lord's coming, we shall find it was to save us from our sins, to be a propitiation for our sins, to give His life a ransom for many. But then, if the benefits of our dear Redeemer's death were to extend no further than barely to procure forgiveness of our sins, we should have as little reason to rejoice in it as a poor condemned criminal that is ready to perish by some fatal disease would have in receiving a pardon from his judge. For Christians would do well to consider that there is not only a legal hindrance to our happiness, as we are breakers of God's law, but also a moral impurity in our natures, which renders us incapable of enjoying heaven (as hath been already proven) 'till some mighty change hath been wrought in us. It is necessary, therefore, in order to make Christ's redemption complete, that we should have a grant of God's Holy Spirit to change our natures, and so prepare us for the enjoyment of that happiness our Savior has purchased by His precious blood.

Accordingly the Holy Scriptures inform us that whom Christ justifies (that is, as we said before, whose sins He forgives), those He also sanctifies, that is, purifies and cleanses and totally changes their corrupted natures. Nay, in one place of Scripture, sanctification is put before justification on purpose, as it were, to convince us that there is no salvation to be had without it: but you are washed, says the apostle, but you are sanctified, and then follows, but you are justified. As the Scripture also speaks in another place, Christ is to us justification, sanctification, and then redemption. Let this therefore be admitted as another indisputable argument why we must be new creatures, ere we can be in Christ, because without it Christ is dead in vain.

Proceed we now to the next general thing proposed, namely, to draw some inferences from what has been delivered.

And first, then, if he that is in Christ must be a new creature, this may serve as a reproof for some who rest in a bare performance of outward duties, without perceiving any real inward change of heart.

We may observe a great many persons to be very punctual in the regular returns of public and private prayer, as likewise of receiving the Holy Communion and, perhaps now and then too, in keeping a fast. And so far we grant they do well. But here is the misfortune: they rest barely in the use of the means and think all is over when they have just complied with these sacred institutions. Whereas, were they rightly informed they would consider that all the instituted means of grace as prayer, fasting, hearing and reading the word of God, receiving the blessed sacrament, and such like are no further serviceable to us than as they are found to make us inwardly better and to carry on the spiritual life in the soul.

It is true they are means, and essential ones too, but they are only means; they are part but not the whole of religion. For if |not| so, who |was| more religious than the Pharisee, who fasted twice in the week, who gave tithes of all that he possessed, and yet was not justified, as our Savior himself informs us, in the sight of God?

You, perhaps, like the Pharisee, may fast often and make long prayers. You may, with Herod, hear good sermons gladly; or, as Judas himself in all probability did, receive the blessed sacrament. But yet, if you continue vain and trifling, immoral or worldly-minded in your conversations, and differ from the rest of your neighbors barely in going to church or in complying with some outward performances, are you better than they? No, in no wise. You are by far much worse, because those that wholly neglect the means are answerable only for omitting the use of God's ordinances; whereas if you use them, and at the same time abuse them by not letting them produce their intended effect, you thereby encourage others to think there is nothing in them, and therefore must expect to "receive the greater damnation."

But, secondly, if he that is in Christ must be a new creature, then this may check the groundless presumption of another class of professors who rest in the attainment of some moral virtues and falsely imagine they are good Christians if they are just in their dealings, are temperate in their diet, and do hurt or violence to no man.

But if this was all that is requisite to make us Christians, why might not the heathens of old be good Christians, who were remarkable for these virtues, or St. Paul, before his conversation, who tells us that then he lived in all good conscience and was, touching the law, blameless. And yet, after his conversion, we find he renounces all dependence on works of this nature and only desires to be found in Christ, and to know the power of His resurrection, that is, to have an experimental proof of receiving the Holy Ghost, purchased for him by the death and ensured and applied to him by the resurrection of Jesus Christ.

The sum of the matter is this: Christianity includes morality, as grace does reason. But if we are only mere moralists, if we are not inwardly wrought upon and changed by the powerful operations of the Holy Spirit, and |if| our moral actions |do not| proceed from a principle of a new nature, however we may call ourselves Christians, it is to be feared we shall be found naked at the Great Day, and in the number of those who vainly depend on their own righteousness, and not on the righteousness of Jesus Christ imputed to and inherent in them, as necessary to their eternal salvation.

Nor, thirdly, will this doctrine less condemn those who rest in a partial amendment of themselves, without going on to perfection and experiencing a thorough, real, inward change of heart.

A little acquaintance with the world will furnish us with instances of no small number of persons who perhaps were before openly profane but, seeing the ill consequences of their vice and the many worldly inconveniences it has reduced them to, on a sudden, as it were, grow civilized and thereupon flatter themselves that they are very religious because they differ a little from their former selves and are not so scandalously wicked as once they were. Whereas at the same time they shall have some secret darling sin or other, some beloved Delilah or Herodias, which they will not part with, some hidden lust which they will not mortify, some vicious habit which they will not take pains to root out. But would you know, O vain man, whoever you are, what the Lord your God requires of you? You must be informed that nothing short of a thorough, sound conversion will avail for the salvation of your soul. It is not enough to turn from profaneness to civility, but you must turn from civility to godliness. Not only some, but all things must become new in your soul. It will profit you but little to do many things, if yet some one thing you lack. In short, you must not be only an almost but altogether a new creature, or in vain you hope for a saving interest in Christ.

Fourthly and lastly, if he that is in Christ must be a new creature, then this may be prescribed as an infallible rule for every person of whatever denomination, age, degree, or quality to judge himself by, this being the only solid foundation whereon we can build a well-grounded assurance of pardon, peace, and happiness.

We may indeed depend on the broken reed of an external profession. We may think we have done enough if we lead such sober, honest, moral lives as many heathens did. We may imagine we are in a safe condition if we attend on the public offices of religion and are constant in the duties of our closets. But unless all these tend to reform our lives and change our hearts and are only used as so many channels of divine grace, as I told you before so I tell you again, Christianity will profit us nothing.

Let each of us therefore seriously put this question to our hearts: have we received the Holy Ghost since we believed? Are we new creatures in Christ, or no? At least, if we are not so yet, is it our daily endeavor to become such? Do we make a constant and conscientious use of all the means of grace required thereto? Do we fast, watch, and pray? Do we not only lazily seek but laboriously strive to enter in at the strait gate? In short, do we renounce ourselves, take up our crosses, and follow Christ? If so, we are in that narrow way which leads to life; we are, at least shall in time become, new creatures in Christ. The good seed is sown in our hearts and will, if duly watered and nourished by a regular persevering use of all the means of grace, grow up to eternal life. But on the contrary, if we have only *heard* and know not experimentally whether there be any Holy Ghost; if we are strangers to fasting, watching, and prayer, and all the other spiritual exercises of devotion; if we are content to go in the broad way merely because we see most other people do so, without once reflecting whether it be the right one or not; in short, if we are strangers, nay enemies to the cross of Christ, by leading lives of softness, worldly-mindedness, and sensual pleasure, and thereby make others think that Christianity is but an empty name, a bare formal profession—if this be the case, I say, then Christ is as yet dead in vain as to us. We are yet under the guilt of our sins; we are unacquainted with that true and thorough conversion which alone can entitle us to the salvation of our souls.

But, beloved, I am persuaded better things of you, and things that accompany salvation, though we thus speak, and humbly hope that you are fully and heartily convinced that nothing but the wedding garment of a new nature can gain admission for you at the marriage feast of the supper of the lamb; that you are sincerely persuaded that he that has not the Spirit of Christ is none of His, and that unless the Spirit which raised Jesus from the dead dwell in you here neither will your mortal bodies be quickened by the same Spirit to dwell with Him hereafter.

Let me therefore (as we proposed in the last place) earnestly exhort you in the name of our Lord Jesus Christ to act suitable to those convictions, and to live as Christians, that are commanded in Holy Writ to put off their former conversation concerning the old man and to put on the new man, which is created after God, in righteousness and true holiness.

It must be owned indeed that this is a great and difficult work but, blessed be God, it is not impossible. Many thousands of happy souls have been assisted by a divine power to bring it about, and why should we despair of success? Is God's hand shortened, that it cannot save? Was He the God of our fathers, is He not the God of their children also? Yes, doubtless of their children also.

It is a task likewise that will put us to some pain. It will oblige us to part with some lust, to break with some friend, to mortify some beloved passion which may be exceeding dear to us, and perhaps as hard to leave as to cut off a right hand or to pluck out a right eye. But what of all this? Will not the being made a real living member of Christ, a child of God and an inheritor of the kingdom of heaven, abundantly make amends for all this trouble? Undoubtedly it will.

Lastly, setting about and carrying on this great and necessary work perhaps may, nay, assuredly will expose us to the ridicule of the unthinking part of mankind, who will wonder that we run not into the same excess of riot with themselves. And because we may deny our sinful appetites and are not conformed to this world, being commanded in Scripture to do the one and to have our conversation in heaven in opposition to the other, they may count our lives folly and our end to be without honor. But will not the being numbered among the saints and shining as the stars for ever and ever be a more than sufficient recompense for all the ridicule, calumny, or reproach we can possibly meet with here?

Indeed, were there no other reward attending a thorough conversion but that peace of God which is the unavoidable consequence of it and which, even in this life, passes all understanding, we should have great reason to rejoice. But when we consider this is the least of those mercies God has prepared for those that are in Christ new creatures, that this is but the beginning of an eternal succession of pleasures, that the day of our deaths, which the unconverted, unrenewed sinner must so much dread, will be, as it were, but the first day of our new births and open to us an everlasting scene of happiness and comfort— in short, if we remember that they who are regenerate and born again have a real title to all the glorious promises of the gospel and are infallibly certain of being as happy, both here and hereafter, as an all-wise, all-gracious, all-powerful God can make them, methinks every one that has but the least concern for the salvation of his precious, his immortal soul, having such promises, such an hope, such an eternity of happiness set before him, should never cease watching, praying, and striving till he find a real, inward, saving change wrought in his heart, and thereby knows of a truth that he dwells in Christ and Christ in him; that he is a new creature in Christ; that he is therefore a child of God; that he is already an inheritor and will ere long, if he endure to the end, be an actual possessor of the kingdom of heaven.

Which God of His infinite mercy grant, through Jesus Christ our Lord, "to whom |be glory and honor, power and dominion, world without end. Amen."|

SALVATION BY FAITH

by John Wesley

(A Sermon preached at St. Mary's, Oxford, before the University, on June 11, 1738)

INTRODUCTION

In this, his first published sermon, you can see Wesley the theologian, just two weeks after Aldersgate, carefully but joyfully laying out the arguments for regeneration by grace, through faith in Christ. He had been proclaiming the promise of it for the past two months, since his reading of the Book of Acts had persuaded him that Peter Böhler was right about an instant of saving faith which brought deliverance from both the guilt and power of sin.

The reader can use this sermon to test whether Luke L. Keefer was correct in reemphasizing recently that Aldersgate was indeed the central turning point in Wesley's religion. From that day forward, Keefer says, John Wesley turned away from teaching that good works, the sacraments, and membership in the church were the way to salvation and the post-apostolic fathers the chief source of truth about it. Thereafter, he stressed continually the notion of salvation by faith in Christ; and the New Testament was his principal authority.

This sermon has no reference at all to the early church fathers, but is jam-packed with quotations from the Holy Scriptures, especially from the New Testament, concerning the faith through which we, by grace, may enjoy a present salvation. In it, Wesley is clearly seeking to evangelize, that is, to persuade his hearers to accept the doctrine and to believe on Christ for themselves. His only reference to tradition is, in fact, to "that glorious champion of the Lord of hosts, Martin Luther," whom he credits for reviving the idea of salvation by faith during the Protestant Reformation. Two years after preaching this sermon, Wesley was to discover and denounce antinomian tendencies in Luther's preface to the commentary on the Galatians. He included that denunciation in a letter to all his preachers; months later, he extended that warning to all who would read his published *Journal* for that date.

More immediately, this sermon reveals how much Wesley felt his responsibility, when preaching before Oxford University, to reason out his points carefully, even though couching them in the words of Scripture. His experience was already troubled; he found the joy he had expected had been relatively short-lived and the severity of his temptations, coming from without and within, was much more than he had anticipated. He spoke as an Anglican, but as one who had discovered scriptural truth. What he had previously believed—that a righteous life was the condition of that justification which Christians would experience at the Judgment Day—gave way to the assurance of being justified now, and by simple faith, of being forgiven and renewed in the image of the Creator.

Here, however, is the same doctrine with which George Whitefield had set much of England aflame. Clearly, Wesley was far more effective at explaining to a community of scholars the scriptural sources and meaning of his doctrine than in presenting the kind of appeal for which Whitefield had already become famous among the masses. But their evangelistic purpose and their theological insights were the same.

❖   ❖   ❖

"By grace you are saved through faith" (Ephesians 2:8).

1. All the blessings which God has bestowed upon man are of his mere grace, bounty, or favor—his free, undeserved favor, favor altogether undeserved, man having no claim to the least of his mercies. It was free grace that "formed man of the dust of the ground, and breathed into him a living soul," and stamped on that soul the image of God, and "put all things under his feet." The same free grace continues to us at this day life, and breath, and all things. For there is nothing we are, or have, or do which can deserve the least thing at God's hand. "All our works you, O God, have wrought in us." These therefore are so many more instances of free mercy: and whatever righteousness may be found in man, this also is the gift of God.

2. Wherewithal then shall a sinful man atone for any the least of his sins? With his own works? No. Were they ever so many or holy, they are not his own but God's. But indeed they are all unholy and sinful themselves, so that every one of them

needs a fresh atonement. Only corrupt fruit grows on a corrupt tree. And his heart is altogether corrupt and abominable, being "come short of the glory of God," the glorious righteousness at first impressed on his soul, after the image of his great Creator. Therefore having nothing, neither righteousness nor works, to plead, his "mouth is utterly stopped before God."

3. If then sinful man find favor with God, it is "grace upon grace" (κάρις ἀντὶ κάριτος). If God vouchsafe still to pour fresh blessings upon us—yea, the greatest of all blessings, *salvation* — what can we say to these things but "Thanks be unto God for His unspeakable gift!" And thus it is. Herein "God commends His love toward us in that, while we were yet sinners, Christ died" to save us. "By grace," then, "are you saved through faith." Grace is the source, faith the condition of salvation.

Now, that we fall not short of the grace of God, it concerns us carefully to inquire:

    I. What faith it is through which we are saved?

    II. What is the salvation which is through faith?

    III. How we may answer some objections.

I. What faith it is through which we are saved.

1. And, first, it is not barely the faith of a heathen. Now God requires of a heathen to believe "that God is, and that He is a rewarder of them that diligently seek Him," and that He is to be sought by "glorifying Him as God, by giving Him thanks" for all things, and by a careful practice of moral virtue, of justice, mercy, and truth toward their fellow-creatures. A Greek or Roman, therefore, yea, a Scythian or Indian, was without excuse if he did not believe thus much: the being and attributes of God, a future state of reward and punishment, and the obligatory nature of moral virtue. For this is barely the faith of a heathen.

2. Nor, secondly, is it the faith of a devil, though this goes much further than that of a heathen. For the devil believes not only that there is a wise and powerful God, gracious to reward and just to punish, but also that Jesus is the Son of God, the Christ, the Savior of the world. So we find him declaring in express terms (Luke 4:34). "I know You who You are, the Holy One of God." Nor can we doubt but that unhappy spirit believes all those words which came out of the mouth of the Holy One, yea, and whatsoever else was written by those holy men of old, of two of whom he was compelled to give that glorious testimony, "These men are the servants of the most high God, who show unto you the way of salvation." This much then the great enemy of God and man believes, and trembles in believing, that "God was made manifest in the flesh," that He will "tread all enemies under His feet," and that "all Scripture was given by inspiration of God." Thus far goes the faith of a devil.

3. Thirdly, the faith through which we are saved, in that sense of the word which will hereafter be explained, is not barely that which the apostles themselves had while Christ was yet upon earth, though they so believed on Him then as to "leave all to follow Him." They had then power to work miracles, "to heal all manner of sickness and all manner of disease." Yea, they had then "power and authority over all devils" and, which is beyond all this, were sent by their Master to "preach the kingdom of God." Yet after their return from doing all these mighty works their Lord himself terms them "a faithless generation" (Luke 9:41). He tells them "they could not cast out a devil because of their unbelief." And when, long after (Luke 17:5), supposing they had some already, they said unto Him, "Increase our faith," He tells them plainly that of this faith they had none at all, no, not as a grain of mustard seed. "The Lord said, If you had faith as a grain of mustard seed, you might say unto this sycamine tree, 'Be plucked up by the roots, and be planted in the sea,' and it should obey you."

4. What faith is it then through which we are saved? It may be answered, first, in general, it is a faith in Christ. Christ, and God through Christ, are the proper object of it. Herein therefore it is sufficiently, absolutely distinguished from the faith either of ancient or modern heathens. And from the faith of a devil it is fully distinguished by this: it is not barely a speculative, rational thing, a cold, lifeless assent, a train of ideas in the head, but also a disposition of the heart. For thus says the Scripture, "With the heart man believes unto righteousness." And, "If you will confess with your mouth the Lord Jesus, and shall believe in your *heart* that God has raised Him from the dead, you shall be saved."

5. And herein does it differ from that faith which the

apostles themselves had while our Lord was on earth, that it acknowledges the necessity and merit of His death and the power of His resurrection. It acknowledges His death as the sufficient, the only sufficient means of redeeming man from death eternal and His resurrection as the restoration of us all to life and immortality, inasmuch as "He was delivered for our sins, and rose again for our justification." Christian faith is then not only an assent to the whole gospel of Christ but also a full reliance on the blood of Christ, a trust in the merits of his life, death, and resurrection. [It is] a recumbency upon Him as our atonement and our life, as *given for us* and *living in us*. It is a confidence in the goodness of God through the Son of His love, living, dying, and interceding for us. It is a closing with Him and cleaving to Him as our "wisdom, righteousness, sanctification, and redemption," or, in one word, our salvation.

II. What salvation it is which is through this faith, is the second thing to be considered.

1. And first, whatsoever else it imply, it is a present salvation. It is something attainable, yea, actually attained on earth, by those who are partakers of this faith. For thus says the apostle to the believers at Ephesus, and in them to the believers of all ages, not, "You shall be" (though that also is true), but "you *are* saved through faith."

2. You are saved (to comprise all in one word) from sin. This is the salvation which is through faith. This is that great salvation foretold by the angel before God brought His first-begotten into the world: "You shall call his name Jesus, for He shall save His people from their sins." And neither here nor in other parts of Holy Writ is there any limitation or restriction. All His people, or as it is elsewhere expressed, all that believe in Him, He will save from all their sins: from original and actual, past and present sin, of the flesh and of the spirit. Through faith that is in Him they are saved both from the guilt and from the power of it.

3. First, from the guilt of all past sin. For whereas all the world is guilty before God (insomuch that should He "be extreme to mark what is done amiss there is none that could abide it"), and whereas "by the law is only the knowledge of sin" but no deliverance from it (so that "by fulfilling the deeds of the law no flesh can be justified in His sight"), now "the righteousness of God, which is by faith of Jesus Christ," "is manifested unto all that believe." Now they are "justified freely by His grace through the redemption that is in Jesus Christ. Him God has set forth to be a propitiation through faith in His blood, to declare His righteousness for (or by) the remission of the sins that are past." Now has Christ "taken away the curse of the law, being made a curse for us." He has "blotted out the handwriting that was against us, taking it out of the way, nailing it to His cross." "There is therefore no condemnation now to them" which believe in Christ Jesus.

4. And being saved from guilt, they are saved from fear. Not indeed from a filial fear of offending but from all servile fear, from that "fear which hath torment," from fear of punishment, from fear of the wrath of God, whom they now no longer regard as a severe master but as an indulgent Father. "They have not received again that spirit of bondage but the Spirit of adoption, whereby they cry, 'Abba, Father,' the Spirit itself also bearing witness with their spirit, that they are the children of God." They are also saved from the fear, though not from the possibility, of falling away from the grace of God and coming short of the great and precious promises. They are "sealed with the Holy Spirit of promise, which is the earnest of their inheritance" (Eph. 1:13). Thus have they "peace with God through our Lord Jesus Christ." They "rejoice in hope of the glory of God." "And the love of God is shed abroad in their hearts through the Holy Ghost which is given unto them." And hereby they are "persuaded" (though perhaps not all at all times, nor with the same fullness of persuasion) that "neither death, nor life, nor things present, nor things to come, nor height, nor depth, nor any other creature shall be able to separate them from the love of God, which is in Christ Jesus our Lord."

5. Again, through this faith they are saved from the power of sin as well as from the guilt of it. Indeed, "the infection of nature remains, which has in itself the nature of sin."* For it is a "coming short of the glory of God." And St. John accordingly declares not

---

*In later editions, Wesley omitted this and the following six and one-half sentences, down to the word *apostle*—the longest omission by far of any he made from the original text of this sermon.

only that if a man "says that he has not sinned he makes God a liar," but also, "If we say we have no sin" now remaining, we deceive ourselves." Many infirmities likewise do remain, whereby we are daily subject to what are called sins of infirmity. And doubtless they are in some sense sins, as being "transgressions of the 'perfect' law." And with regard to these, it may be said of us all our lives that "in many things we offend all." But this notwithstanding, the same apostle declares, "You know that He was manifested to take away our sins, and in Him is no sin. Whosoever abides in Him does not sin" (chap. 3:5ff). Again, "Little children, let no man deceive you. . . . He that commits sin is of the devil." "Whosoever believes is born of God." And "whosoever is born of God does not commit sin, for His seed remains in him; and he cannot sin, because he is born of God." Once more, "We know that whosoever is born of God does not sin; but he that is begotten of God keeps himself, and that wicked one touches him not" (chap. 5:18).

6. He that is by faith born of God does not sin, (1), by any habitual sin; for all habitual sin is sin reigning, but sin cannot reign in any that believes. Nor, (2), by any willful sin; for his will while he abides in the faith is utterly set against all sin, and abhors it as deadly poison. Nor, (3), by any sinful desire; for he continually desires the holy and perfect will of God, and any tendency to an unholy desire he by the grace of God stifles in the birth. Nor, (4), does he sin by infirmities, whether in act, word, or thought; for his infirmities have no concurrence of his will, and without this they are not properly sins. Thus, "he that is born of God has sin in him" but "does not commit sin." And though he cannot say he "has not sinned," yet now "he sins not."

7. This then is the salvation which is through faith, even in the present world: a salvation from sin and the consequences of sin, both often expressed in the word "justification." Which, taken in the largest sense, implies a deliverance from guilt and punishment, by the atonement of Christ actually applied to the soul of the sinner now believing on Him, and a deliverance from the whole body of sin, through Christ gradually "formed in his heart." So that he who is justified or saved by faith is indeed "born again." He is "born again of the Spirit" unto a new life "which is hid with Christ in God." "He is a new creature. Old things are passed away; all things in him are become new." And as a "newborn babe he gladly receives the (ἄδολον) sincere milk of the word, and grows thereby," "going on in the might of the Lord his God," "from faith to faith," "from grace to grace," "until at length he comes unto a perfect man, unto the measure of the stature of the fullness of Christ."

III. The first usual objection to this is,

1. That to preach salvation or justification by faith only is to preach against holiness and good works. To which a short answer might be given: it would be so if we spoke, as some do, of a faith which was exclusive of these. But we speak of a faith which is necessarily inclusive of all good works and all holiness.

2. But it may be of use to consider it more at large, especially since it is no new objection, but as old as St. Paul's time. For even then it was asked, "Do we not make void the law through faith?" We answer first, all who preach not faith do manifestly make void the law, either directly and grossly, by limitations and comments that eat out all the spirit of the text, or indirectly, by not pointing out the only means whereby it is possible to perform it. Whereas, secondly, "we establish the law," both by showing its full extent and spiritual meaning and by calling all to that living way whereby "the righteousness of the law may be fulfilled in them." These, while they trust in the blood of Christ alone, use all the ordinances which He has appointed, do all the "good works which He had before prepared that they should walk therein," and enjoy and manifest all holy and heavenly tempers, even the same "mind that was in Christ Jesus our Lord."

3. But does not preaching this faith lead men into pride? We answer, accidentally it may. Therefore ought every believer to be earnestly cautioned (in the words of the great apostle): "Because of unbelief the first branches were broken off," and "you stand by faith. Be not high-minded, but fear. If God spared not the natural branches, take heed lest He spare not you. Behold therefore the goodness and severity of God: on them which fell, severity, but toward you, goodness, if you continue in His goodness. Otherwise you also shall be cut off." And while he

continues therein, he will remember those words of St. Paul, foreseeing and answering this very objection (Rom. 3:27): "Where is boasting, then? It is excluded. By what law? Of works? Nay, but by the law of faith."

If a man were justified by his works, he would have whereof to glory. But there is no glorying for him "that works not, but believes on Him that justifies the ungodly" (Rom. 4:5). To the same effect are the words both preceding and following the text (Eph. 2:4ff): "God, who is rich in mercy, . . . even when we were dead in sins, has quickened us together with Christ (by grace you are saved), . . . that He might show the exceeding riches of His grace in His kindness toward us through Christ Jesus. For by grace you are saved through faith, and that not of yourselves." Of yourselves comes neither your faith nor your salvation. "It is the gift of God," the free, undeserved gift—the faith through which you are saved, as well as the salvation which He of His own good pleasure, His mere favor, annexes thereto.

That you believe is one instance of His grace; that believing, you are saved, another. "Not of works, lest any man should boast." For all our works, all our righteousness, which were before our believing, merited nothing of God but condemnation, so far were they from deserving faith, which therefore, whenever given, is not "of works." Neither is salvation of the works we do when we believe. For "it is" then "God that works in us." And therefore, that He gives us a reward for what He Himself works only commends the riches of His mercy, but leaves us nothing whereof to glory.

4. However, may not the speaking thus of the mercy of God, as saving or justifying freely by faith only, encourage men in sin? Indeed it may and will; many will "continue in sin, that grace may abound." But their blood is upon their own head. The goodness of God ought to lead them to repentance, and so it will those who are sincere of heart. When they know there is yet forgiveness with Him, they will cry aloud that He would blot out their sins also through faith which is in Jesus. And if they earnestly cry and faint not, if they seek Him in all the means He has appointed, if they refuse to be comforted till He come, He "will come, and will not tarry." And He can do much work in a short time. Many are the examples in the Acts of the Apostles of God's shedding abroad this faith in men's hearts even like lightning falling from heaven. So in the same hour that Paul and Silas began to preach the jailer "repented, believed, and was baptized," as were three thousand by St. Peter on the day of Pentecost, who all repented and believed at his first preaching. And, blessed be God, there are now many living proofs that He is still "mighty to save."

5. Yet to the same truth, placed in another view, a quite contrary objection is made: "If a man cannot be saved by *all that he can do*, this will drive men to *despair* ." True, to despair of being saved by their own works, their own merits or righteousness. And so it ought; for none can trust in the merits of Christ till he has utterly renounced his own. He that "goes about to establish his own righteousness" cannot receive the righteousness of God. The righteousness which is of faith cannot be given him while he trusts in that which is of the law.

6. But this, it is said, is an uncomfortable doctrine. The devil spoke like himself, that is, without either truth or shame, when he dared to suggest to men that it is such. 'Tis the only comfortable one, 'tis "very full of comfort" to all self-destroyed, self-condemned sinners. That "whosoever believes on Him shall not be ashamed"; that "the same Lord over all is rich unto all that call upon Him"—here is comfort, high as heaven, stronger than death!

What, mercy for all? For Zaccheus, a public robber? For Mary Magdalene, a common harlot? Methinks I hear one say, "Then I, even I, may hope for mercy!" And so you may, you afflicted one, whom none has comforted! God will not cast out your prayer. Nay, perhaps He may say the next hour, "Be of good cheer, your sins are forgiven you"—so forgiven that they shall reign over you no more, yea, and that "the Holy Spirit shall bear witness with your spirit that you are a child of God." O glad tidings! Tidings of great joy, which are sent unto all people. "Ho, everyone that thirsts, come to the waters; come and buy without money and without price." Whatsoever your sins be, "though red, like crimson," though "more than the hairs of your head," "return unto the Lord, and He will have mercy upon you, and to our God, for He will abundantly pardon."

7. When no more objections occur, then we are simply told that justification by faith only ought not to be preached as the

first doctrine, or at least not to be preached to all. But what says the Holy Ghost? "Other foundation can no man lay than that which is laid, even Jesus Christ." So, then, "that whosoever believes on Him shall be saved" is and must be the foundation of all our preaching, that is, must be preached first. "Well, but not to all." To whom then are we not to preach it? Whom shall we except? The poor? Nay, they have a peculiar right to have the gospel preached unto them. The unlearned? No. God has revealed these things unto unlearned and ignorant men from the beginning. The young? By no means. "Suffer these" in any wise "to come unto Christ, and forbid them not." The sinners? Least of all. He "came not to call the righteous, but sinners to repentance." Why then, if any, we are to except the rich, the learned, the reputable, the moral men. And 'tis true, they too often except themselves from hearing; yet we must speak the words of our Lord. For thus the tenor of our commission runs: "Go and preach the gospel to every creature." If any man wrest it or any part of it to his destruction, he must bear his own burden. But still, "as the Lord lives, whatsoever the Lord says unto us, that we will speak."

8. At this time more especially will we speak that "by grace you are saved through faith," because never was the maintaining this doctrine more seasonable than it is at this day. Nothing but this can effectually prevent the increase of the Romish delusion among us. 'Tis endless to attack one by one all the errors of that apostate Church. But salvation by faith strikes at the root, and all fall at once where this is established. It was this doctrine (which our church justly calls "the strong rock and foundation of the Christian religion") that first drove popery out of these kingdoms, and 'tis this alone can keep it out. Nothing but this can give a check to that immorality which has "overspread our land as a flood." Can you empty the great deep, drop by drop? Then you may reform us by dissuasives from particular vices. But let "the righteousness which is of God by faith" be brought in, and so shall its proud waves be stayed. Nothing but this can stop the mouths of those who "glory in their shame" and "openly deny the Lord that bought them." They can talk |as| sublimely of the law as he that has it written by God in his heart. To hear them speak on this head might incline one to think they were not far from the kingdom of God. But take them out of the law into the gospel;

begin with the righteousness of faith, with "Christ, the end of the law to everyone that believes"; and those who but now appeared almost if not altogether Christians stand confessed the sons of perdition, as far from life and salvation (God be merciful unto them!) as the depth of hell from the height of heaven.

9. For this reason the adversary so rages whenever "salvation by faith" is declared to the world. For this reason did he stir up earth and hell to destroy those who first preached it. And for the same reason, knowing that faith alone could overturn the foundations of his kingdom, did he call forth all his force and employ all his arts of lies and calumny to affright that glorious champion of the Lord of Hosts, Martin Luther, from reviving it. Nor can we wonder thereat. For as that man of God observes, "How would it enrage a proud strong man armed to be stopped and set at nought by a little child, coming against him with a reed in his hand!"—especially when he knew that little child would surely overthrow him and tread him under foot. "Even so, Lord Jesus!" Thus has your strength been ever "made perfect in weakness"! Go forth then, you little child that believes in Him, and His "right hand shall teach you terrible things!" Though you are helpless and weak as an infant of days, the strong man shall not be able to stand before you. You shall prevail over him, and subdue him, and overthrow him, and trample him under your feet. You shall march on under the great Captain of your salvation, "conquering and to conquer," until all your enemies are destroyed and "death is swallowed up in victory."

Now thanks be to God who gives us the victory through our Lord Jesus Christ, to whom, with the Father and the Holy Ghost, be blessing, and glory, and wisdom, and thanksgiving, and honor, and power, and might, for ever and ever. Amen.

THE INDWELLING OF
THE SPIRIT, THE COMMON
PRIVILEGE OF
ALL BELIEVERS

by George Whitefield

INTRODUCTION

This sermon represents the blossoming of Whitefield's powers of persuasion. It also reveals the full development of his theology. To read it is to be convinced of the folly of those who, then as in recent times, have thought of Whitefield as primarily an enthusiast and not as one who understood biblical teachings.

His doctrines are set forth here in scriptural terms, and always with the intention of persuading Whitefield's Anglican audience. This was no doubt the reason the sermon pleased John Wesley and made him eager to assist Whitefield in editing and preparing it for publication. Late in June, 1739, when they edited this sermon, the two men were preaching their way together through central England, at a time when scholars have alleged they were estranged on account of Wesley's sermon against predestination at Bristol, two months earlier!

The sermon takes the offensive against Anglican ministers who denied that believers can be conscious of the Holy Spirit's presence in their lives. Quoting passages from the church's *Book of Common Prayer* as well as from the Scriptures, Whitefield came to his climax in a denunciation of clergymen who were not loyal to the creeds of their own communion. John Wesley must have rejoiced. The argument anticipates much that Wesley wrote four years later in his *Appeal to Men of Reason and Religion*, the first and last sections of which appear later in this volume.

Also, Whitefield's explanation of the fall of humankind in Adam summarizes a doctrine to which John Wesley was deeply attached. The young evangelist's language was not circumspect but his argument resembled one which Wesley made on many occasions, especially in his volume on original sin. Both men thought that the fact of "inbred sin" made necessary the promise of the gift of the Holy Spirit to give us freedom from its dominion. The pathos of Whitefield's long appeal to his hearers to let that promise be fulfilled in their own lives shows how difficult it is to separate either man's evangelism from his theology, or both man's thought and methods from scriptural authority.

Here, then, is an emotionally satisfying way to come to grips with the central doctrine of the evangelical awakening, that of the gift of the Holy Spirit to those who are born again. During these early years Whitefield and Wesley both thought that inward corruption would remain in all Christians, and only be gradually uprooted by the sanctifying Spirit. Wesley, however, came a few months later to believe that to be "filled" with the same Holy Spirit, in a second moment of faith, meant to be cleansed of that corruption. For these brief months, however, they were in complete harmony. On the idea of the new birth, evangelicals always have been.

The sermon was republished at once in Boston, and in Philadelphia and Williamsburg the next year. The copy I have used below is from the original London and Edinburgh edition, published a few weeks after Pentecost Sunday, 1739, when the young evangelist delivered it. The American editions show how fully the doctrines of the evangelical awakening were transmitted to the United States, where Whitefield became an immensely popular preacher.

❖   ❖   ❖

"In the last day, that great day of the feast, Jesus stood and cried, saying, If any man thirsts, let him come unto me, and drink. He that believes on me, as the Scripture has said, out of his belly shall flow rivers of living water. But this spoke He of the Spirit, which they that believe on Him should receive" (John 7:37–39).

Nothing has rendered the cross of Christ of less effect, nothing has been a greater stumbling block and rock of offense to weak minds, than a supposition now current among us that most of what is contained in the gospel of Jesus Christ was designed only for our Lord's first and immediate followers and consequently calculated for one or two hundred years. Accordingly many now read the life, sufferings, death, and resurrection of Jesus Christ in the same manner as learned men read Caesar's *Commentaries* or the *Conquests of Alexander*, as things rather intended to afford matter for speculation than to be acted over again in and by us.

As this is true of the doctrines of the gospel in general, so it is in particular of the operations of God's Spirit upon the hearts of believers. For we no sooner mention the necessity of our receiving the Holy Ghost in these last days, as well as formerly, but we are looked upon by some as enthusiasts and madmen, and by others represented as willfully deceiving the people and undermining the established constitution of the church.

Judge you then, my brethren, whether it is not high time for the true ministers of Jesus Christ, who have been themselves made partakers of this heavenly gift, to lift up their voices like a trumpet and, if they would not have those souls perish for which the Lord Jesus has shed His precious blood, to declare with all boldness that the Holy Spirit is the common privilege and portion of all believers in all ages, and that we also, as well as the first Christians, must receive the Holy Ghost ere we can be truly called the children of God.

For this reason, and also that I might answer the design of our church in appointing the present festival [of Pentecost], I have chosen the words of the text.

They were spoken by Jesus Christ when, as the evangelist tells us, He was at the feast of tabernacles. Our Lord (herein lending all an example) attended the temple service in general and the festivals of the Jewish church in particular. The festival at which He was now present . . . the Jews observed, according to God's appointment, in commemoration of their living in tents. At the last day of this feast it was customary for many pious people to fetch water from a certain place and bring it on their heads, singing this anthem out of Isaiah: "And with joy shall they draw water out of the wells of salvation." Our dear Lord Jesus observing this, and it being His constant practice to spiritualize everything He met with, cries out, If any man thirst, let him come unto me, rather than unto that well, and drink. "He that believeth on me, as the Scripture has spoken (where it is said, God will make water spring out of a dry rock, and such like), out of his belly shall flow rivers of living water." And that we might know what our Savior meant by this living water, the evangelist immediately adds, "But this spoke He of the Spirit, which they that believe on Him should receive."

These last words I shall chiefly insist on in the ensuing discourse, and shall treat on them in the following manner:

First, I shall briefly show what is meant by the word Spirit.

Secondly, I shall show that this Spirit is the common privilege of all believers.

Thirdly, I shall show the reason on which this doctrine is founded.

Lastly, I shall conclude with a general exhortation to believe on Jesus Christ, whereby alone we can be qualified to receive this Spirit.

And *first*, I am briefly to show what is meant by the Spirit.

By the Spirit, or the Holy Ghost, is to be understood the third person in the ever blessed Trinity, consubstantial and coeternal with the Father and the Son, proceeding from, yet equal to them both. For, to use the words of our church in this day's office, that which we believe of the glory of the Father, the same we believe of the Son and of the Holy Ghost, without any difference or inequality.

Thus says St. John in his first Epistle, chapter 5, verse 7: "There are three that bear record in heaven," the Father, the Word, and the Holy Ghost; "and these three are one." And our Lord, when He gave His apostles commission to go and teach all nations, commanded them to baptize in the name of the Holy Ghost, as well as of the Father and the Son. And St. Peter, Acts 5:3, said to Ananias, "Why has Satan filled your heart to lie to the Holy Ghost?" And [in] verse 4 he says, "You have not lied unto men, but unto God." From all which passages it is plain that the Holy Ghost is truly and properly God, as well as the Father and the Son. This is an unspeakable mystery, but a mystery of God's revealing, and therefore to be assented to with our whole hearts, seeing God is not a man that He should lie, nor the son of man that He should deceive.

I proceed *secondly* to prove that the Holy Ghost is the common privilege of all believers.

But here I would not be understood of [our] so receiving the Holy Ghost as to enable us to work miracles or show outward signs and wonders. For I allow our adversaries that to pretend to be inspired in this sense is being wise above what is written. Perhaps it cannot be proved that God ever interposed in this extraordinary manner, . . . [except] when some new revelation was to be established, as at the first settling of the Mosaic and gospel dispensations. And as for my own part, I cannot but suspect the spirit of those who insist upon a repetition of such miracles at this time. For the world being now become nominally Christian, at least (though God knows little of the power is left among us), there need not [be] outward miracles, but only an inward cooperation of the Holy Spirit with the Word, to prove that Jesus is that Messiah which was to come into the world.

Besides, it is possible for you, O man, to have faith, so as to be able to remove mountains or cast out devils; nay, you might speak with the tongue of men and angels, yea, and bid the sun stand still in the midst of heaven; yet, what would all these gifts of the Spirit avail you, without being made partaker of His sanctifying graces? [King] Saul had the spirit of government for awhile, so as to become another man, and yet was a reprobate. And many who cast out devils in Christ's name at the last will be disowned by Him. If therefore you had only the gifts but were destitute of the graces of the Holy Ghost, they would only serve to lead you with so much the more solemnity to hell.

Here then, I say, we join issue with our adversaries, and will readily grant that we are not in this sense to be inspired, as were our Lord's first apostles. But unless men have eyes which see not and ears which hear not, how can they read the latter part of the text and not confess that the Holy Spirit, in another sense, is the common privilege of all believers, even to the end of the world? "This spoke He of the Spirit, which they that believe on Him should receive." Observe, He does not say they that believe on Him for one or two ages, but they that believe on Him in general, that is, at all times and in all places. So that unless we can prove that St. John was under a delusion when he wrote these words, we must believe that we, even we also, shall receive the Holy Ghost, if we believe on the Lord Jesus with our whole hearts.

Again, our Lord, just before His bitter passion, when He was about to offer up His soul an offering for the sins of the world, when His heart was most enlarged and He would undoubtedly demand the most excellent gifts for His disciples, prays that "they all may be one; as You, Father, are in Me, and I in You, that they also may be one in us. I in them, and You in Me, that they be made perfect in one." That is, that all His true followers might be united to Him by His Holy Spirit, by as real, vital, and mystical a union as there is between Jesus Christ and the Father. I say all His true followers. For it is evident from our Lord's own words that He had us and all believers in view, when He put up this prayer: "Neither pray I for these alone, but for them also which shall believe on me through their word." So that, unless we treat our Lord as the high priests did and count Him a blasphemer, we must confess that all who believe in Jesus Christ, through the word or ministration of the apostles, are to be joined to Jesus Christ by being made partakers of the Holy Spirit.

There's a great noise made of late about the word enthusiast, and it has been cast upon the preachers of the gospel as a term of reproach. But every Christian, in the proper sense of the word, must be an enthusiast—that is, must be inspired of God, or have God in him. For who dares say he is a Christian 'til he can say, "God is in me"? St. Peter tells us we have many great and precious promises, that we may be made partakers of the divine nature. Our Lord prays that we may be one, as the Father and He are one. And our own church, in conformity to these texts of Scripture, in her excellent communion office, tells us that those who receive the sacrament worthily "dwell in Christ, and Christ in them; that they are one with Christ, and Christ with them." And yet Christians in general must have their names cast out as evil, and ministers in particular must be looked upon as deceivers of the people, for affirming that we must be really united to God by receiving the Holy Ghost. Be astonished, O heavens, at this!

Indeed, I will not say our letter-learned preachers deny this doctrine in express words. But, however, they do it in effect. For they talk professedly against inward feelings and say we may have God's Spirit without feeling it, which is in reality to deny the thing itself. And had I a mind to hinder the progress of the gospel and to establish the kingdom of darkness, I would go about telling people they might have the Spirit of God and yet not feel it.

But to return, when our Lord was about to ascend to His Father, and our Father, to His God, and our God, He gave His apostles this commission: "Go and teach all nations, baptizing them in the name of the Father, and of the Son, and of the Holy Ghost." By the term "all nations," 'tis allowed, are meant all that should profess to believe on Jesus always, even to the end of the world. And accordingly by authority of this commission, we do baptize them in this and every age of the church. And if this be true, then the proposition to be proved will be undeniable. For though we translate these words, "baptizing them in the name," yet as the name of God, in the Lord's Prayer and several other places, signifies His nature, they might as well be translated thus: "Baptizing into the nature of the Father, into the nature of the Son, and into the nature of the Holy Ghost. And consequently, if we are all to be baptized into the nature of the Holy Ghost ere our baptism be effectual to salvation, it is evident that we all must actually receive the Holy Ghost ere we can say we truly believe in Jesus Christ. For no one can say that "Jesus is *my* Lord" but he that has thus received the Holy Ghost.

Numbers of other texts might be quoted to make this doctrine, if possible, still more plain. But I am astonished that any who call themselves members, much more that many who are preachers of the Church of England, should dare so much as open their lips against it. And yet, with grief, God is my judge, I speak it: persons of the established church seem more generally to be ignorant of it than any dissenters whatsoever.

But good God, my dear brethren, what have you been doing? How often have your hearts given your lips the lie? How often have you offered God the sacrifice of fools and had your prayers turned into sin, if you approve of and use our excellent church liturgy and yet deny the Holy Spirit to be the portion of all believers? In the daily absolution, the minister exhorts the people to pray that God would grant them repentance and His Holy Spirit. In the collect for Christmas day, we beseech God that He would daily renew us by His Holy Spirit. In the last week's collect we prayed that we may evermore rejoice in the comforts of the Holy Ghost. And in the concluding prayer which we put up every day, we pray not only that the grace of our Lord Jesus Christ and the love of God but that the fellowship of the Holy Ghost may be with us all evermore.

But further, a solemn season is now approaching. I mean the Ember days, at the end of which all that are to be ordained to the office of a deacon are, in the sight of God and in the presence of the congregation, to declare that they trust they are inwardly moved by the Holy Ghost to take upon them that administration. And to those who are to be ordained priests, the bishop is to repeat these solemn words, "Receive the Holy Ghost, now committed unto you by the imposition of our hands." And yet (O that I had no reason to speak it) many that use our forms and many that have witnessed this good confession yet dare talk and preach against the necessity of receiving the Holy Ghost now, as well as formerly, and not only so, but cry out against those who do insist upon it as madmen, enthusiasts, schismatics, and underminers of the established constitution.

But you are the schismatics, you are the bane of the Church of England, who are always crying out, "The temple of the Lord, the temple of the Lord," and yet starve the people out of their communion by feeding them only with the dry husks of dead morality and not bringing out to them the fatted calf. I mean the doctrines of the operations of the blessed Spirit of God. But here's the misfortune: many of us are not led by, and therefore no wonder that we cannot talk feelingly of, the Holy Ghost. We subscribe to our articles and make them serve for a key to get into church preferment, and then preach contrary to those very articles to which we have subscribed. Far be it from me to charge all the clergy with this hateful hypocrisy. No, blessed be God, there are some left among us who dare maintain the doctrines of the reformation and preach the truth as it is in Jesus. But I speak the truth in Christ, I lie not, the generality of the clergy are fallen from our articles and do not speak agreeable to them or to the form of sound words delivered in the Scriptures.

Woe be unto such blind leaders of the blind! How can you escape the damnation of hell? It is not all your learning (falsely so called), it is not all your preferments can keep you from the just judgment of God. Yet a little while and we shall all appear before the tribunal of Christ. There, there will I meet you. There Jesus Christ, that great shepherd and bishop of souls, shall determine who are the false prophets, who are the wolves in sheep's clothing—those who say that we must now receive and feel the Holy Ghost, or those who exclaim against it as the doctrine of devils.

But I can [say] no more. It is an unpleasing task to censure any order of men, especially those who are in the ministry. Nor would any thing excuse it but necessity, that necessity which extorted from our Lord himself so many woes against the scribes and Pharisees, the letter-learned rulers and teachers of the Jewish church. And surely, if I could bear to see people perish for lack of knowledge and yet be silent towards those who keep from them the key of true knowledge, the very stones would cry out.

Would we restore the church to its primitive dignity, the only way is to live and preach the doctrine of Christ and the articles to which we have subscribed. Then we shall find the number of dissenters will daily decrease and the Church of England become the joy of the whole earth.

I am now, in the *third* place, to show the reasonableness of this doctrine.

I say, the reasonableness of this doctrine; for however it may seem foolishness to the natural man, yet to those who have tasted of the good word of life and have felt the powers of the world to come, it will appear to be founded on the highest reason and is capable, to those who have eyes to see, even of a demonstration. I say of a demonstration; for it stands on this self-evident supposition, that we are fallen creatures or, to use the Scripture expression, have all died in Adam.

I know indeed 'tis now no uncommon thing among us to deny the doctrine of original sin, as well as the divinity of Jesus Christ, who is God over all, blessed forever. But it is incumbent on those who deny it first to disprove the authority of the Holy Scriptures. If you can prove, you unbeliever, that the book which we call the Bible does not contain the lively oracles of God; if you can show that holy men of old did not write this book, as they were inwardly moved by the Holy Ghost; then will we give up the doctrine of original sin. But unless you can do this, we must insist upon it that we are all conceived and born in sin, if for no other, yet for this one reason, because that God, who cannot lie, has told us so.

But what has light to do with darkness or polite infidels with the Bible? Alas, as they are strangers to the power, so they are generally as great strangers to the Word of God. And therefore, if we will preach to them, we must preach from |our| . . . hearts; for talking in the language of the Scripture is but like talking in an unknown tongue.

14223

Tell me then, O man, whosoever you are that denies the doctrine of original sin, if your conscience be not seared as with a hot iron! Tell me if you do not find yourself by nature to be a motley mixture of brute and devil? I know these terms will stir up the whole Pharisee in your heart; but let not Satan hurry you hence. Stop a little and let us reason together. Do you not find that by nature you are prone to pride? Otherwise, wherefore are you now offended? Again, do you not find in yourself the seeds of malice, revenge, and all uncharitableness? And what are these but the very tempers of the Devil? Again, do we not all by nature follow and suffer ourselves to be led by our natural appetites, always looking downwards, never looking upwards to that God in whom we live, move, and have our being? And what is this but the very nature of the beasts that perish? Out of your own heart therefore will I oblige you to confess what an inspired apostle has long since told us, that the whole world by nature lies in the |grip of the| wicked one, that is, the Devil, that we are no better than those whom St. Jude calls brute beasts. For we have tempers in us all by nature that prove to a demonstration that we are altogether earthly, sensual, devilish.

And this, by the way, will serve as another argument to prove the reality of the operations of the blessed Spirit on the hearts of believers, against those false professors who deny there is any such thing as influences of the Holy Spirit that may be felt. For if they will grant that the Devil works, and that so as to be felt in the hearts of the children of disobedience (which they must grant, unless they will give an apostle the lie), where is the wonder that the good Spirit should have the same power over those that are truly obedient to the faith of Jesus Christ?

But to return. If it be true, then, that we are all by nature a motley mixture of brute and devil, it is evident that we all must receive the Holy Ghost ere we can dwell with and enjoy God.

When you read how the prodigal in the gospel was reduced to so low a condition as to eat husks with swine, and how Nebuchadnezzar was turned out to graze with oxen, I am confident you pity their unhappy state. And when you hear how Jesus Christ will say at the Last Day to all that are not born again of God, "Depart from me, you cursed, into everlasting fire, prepared for the Devil and his angels," do not your hearts shrink within you with a secret horror? And if creatures with only our degree of goodness cannot bear even the thoughts of dwelling with beasts or devils, to whose nature we are so nearly allied, how do we imagine |that| God, who is infinite goodness and purity itself, can dwell with us while we are partakers of both their natures? We might as well think to reconcile heaven and hell.

When Adam had eaten the forbidden fruit he fled and hid himself from God. Why? Because he was naked; that is, he was alienated from the life of God, the due punishment of his disobedience. Now we are all by nature naked and void of God, as he was at that time; and consequently till we are changed and clothed upon by a divine nature again, we must fly from God also.

Hence then appears the reasonableness of our being obliged to receive the Spirit of God. It is founded on the doctrine of original sin. And therefore you will always find that those who talk against feeling the operations of the Holy Ghost very rarely, or very slightly at least, mention our fall in Adam. No, they refer St. Paul's account of the depravity of unbelievers only to those of old time. Whereas 'tis obvious, on the contrary, that we are all equally included under the guilt and consequences of our first parent's sin, even as others, and, to use the language of our own church article, bring into the world with us a corruption which renders us liable to God's wrath and eternal damnation.

Should I preach to you any other doctrine, I should wrong my own soul; I should be found a false witness towards God and you. And he that preaches any other doctrine, howsoever dignified and distinguished, shall bear his punishment, whosoever he be.

From this plain reasoning, then, appears the necessity why we, as well as the first apostles, in this sense must receive the Spirit of God.

For the great work of sanctification, or making us holy, is particularly referred to the Holy Ghost. And therefore our Lord says, "Unless a man be born of the Spirit, he cannot enter into the kingdom of God."

For Jesus Christ came down to save us not only from the guilt but also from the power of sin. And however often we have repeated our creed and told God we believe in the Holy Ghost, yet if we have not believed in Him so as to be really united to

Jesus Christ by Him, we have no more concord with Jesus Christ than Belial himself.

And now, my brethren, what shall I say more? Tell me, are not many of you offended at what has been said already? Do not some of you think, though I mean well, yet I have carried the point a little too far? Are not others ready to cry out, if this be true who then can be saved? Is not this driving people into despair?

Yes, I ingenuously confess it is. But into what despair? A despair of mercy through Christ? No, God forbid; but a despair of living with God without receiving the Holy Ghost. And I would to God that not only all of you that hear me this day but the whole world was filled with this despair. Believe me, my brethren, I have been doing no more than you allow your bodily physicians to do every day. If you have a wound in your bodies and are in earnest about a cure, you bid the surgeon probe it to the very bottom. And shall not the physicians of your soul be allowed the same freedom? And what have I been doing but searching your natural wounds that I might convince you of your danger and put you upon applying to Jesus Christ for a remedy? Indeed I have dealt with you as gently as I could; and now |that| I have wounded, I come to heal you.

For I was, in the *last* place, to exhort you all to come to Jesus Christ by faith, whereby you, even you also, shall receive the Holy Ghost. "For this spoke He of the Spirit, which they that believe on Him should receive."

This, this is what I long to come to. Hitherto I have been preaching only the law, but behold I bring you glad tidings of great joy. If I have wounded you before, be not afraid; behold, I now bring a remedy for all your wounds. For notwithstanding you are all now sunk into the nature of the beast and devil, yet if you truly believe on Jesus Christ you shall receive the quickening Spirit promised in the text, and be restored to the glorious liberties of the sons of God. I say, if you believe on Jesus Christ. For by faith we are saved; it is not of works, lest any one should boast. And however some men may say there is a fitness required in the creature and that we must have a righteousness of our own, before we can lay hold on the righteousness of Christ. Yet, if we believe the Scripture, salvation is the free gift of God in

Christ Jesus our Lord. And whosoever believes on Him with his whole heart, though his soul be as black as hell itself, shall receive the gift of the Holy Ghost.

Behold then, I stand up and cry out in this great day of the feast, let every one that thirsts come unto Jesus Christ and drink. "He that believeth on Him, out of his belly shall flow" not only streams or rivulets, but whole "rivers of living water." This I speak, my brethren, of the Spirit which they that believe on Jesus shall certainly receive. For Jesus Christ is the same yesterday, today, and forever. He is the way, the truth, the resurrection, and the life. Whosoever believeth on Him, though he were dead, yet shall he live. There is no respect of persons with Jesus Christ. High and low, rich and poor, one with another, may come to Him with an humble confidence, if they draw near by faith. From Him we may all receive grace upon grace. For Jesus Christ is full of grace and truth, and ready to save to the uttermost all that by a true faith turn unto Him.

Indeed the poor generally receive the gospel, and God has chosen the poor in this world rich in faith. But though not many mighty, not many noble are called; and though it be "easier for a camel to go through the eye of a needle, than for a rich man to enter into the kingdom of God"; yet even to you that are rich do I now freely offer salvation by Jesus Christ, if you will renounce yourselves and come to Jesus Christ as poor sinners. I say, as poor sinners, for the poor in spirit are only so blessed as to have a right to the kingdom of God. And Jesus Christ calls none to Him but those that thirst after His righteousness and feel themselves weary and heavy laden with the burden of their sins. Jesus Christ justifies the ungodly. He came not to call the righteous but sinners to repentance.

Do not then say you are unworthy; for this is a faithful and true saying, and worthy of all men to be received, that Jesus Christ came into the world to save sinners. And if you are the chief of sinners; if you feel yourselves such, verily Jesus Christ came into the world chiefly to save you. When Joseph was called out of the prison house to Pharaoh's court, we are told that he stayed some time to prepare himself. But do you come with all your prison clothes about you; come poor and miserable and blind and naked as you are; and God the Father shall receive you with open arms, as He did the returning prodigal. He shall cover your nakedness with the best robe of His dear Son's righteousness, shall seal you with the signet of His Spirit, and feed you with the fatted calf, even with the comforts of the Holy Ghost.

Oh let there then be joy in heaven over some of you believing. Let me not go back to my Master and say, "Lord, they will not believe my report." Harden no longer your hearts, but open them wide and let the King of Glory in. Believe me, I am willing to go to prison or death for you; but I am not willing to go to heaven without you. The love of Jesus Christ constrains me to lift up my voice like a trumpet. My heart is now full. Out of the abundance of the love which I have for your precious and immortal souls my mouth now speaks. And I could now not only continue my discourse till midnight, but I could speak till I could speak no more.

And why should I despair of any? No, I can despair of no one, when I consider Jesus Christ has had mercy on such a wretch as I am. However you may think of yourselves, I know that by nature I am but half a devil, and half a beast. The free grace of Christ prevented me. He saw me in my blood. He passed by me and said unto me, "Live." And the same grace which was sufficient for me is sufficient for you also. Behold, the same blessed Spirit is ready to breathe on all your dry bones, if you will believe on Jesus Christ whom God has sent.

Indeed you can never believe on or serve a better master, one that is more mighty or more willing to save. Indeed, I can say the Lord Christ is gracious, His yoke is easy, His burden exceeding light. After you have served Him many years, like the servants under the law, was He willing to discharge you, you would say, "We love our master and will not go from him."

Come then, my guilty brethren, come and believe on the Lord that bought you with His precious blood. Look up by faith and see Him whom you have pierced. Behold Him bleeding, panting, dying! Behold Him with His arms stretched out ready to receive you all. Cry unto Him as the penitent thief did, "Lord, remember us, now You are in Your kingdom"; and He shall say to your souls, "Shortly shall you be with Me in paradise." For those whom Christ justifies, them He also glorifies, even with that glory which He enjoyed with the Father before the world began.

Do not say, "I have bought a piece of ground and must needs go and see it; I have bought a yoke of oxen and must needs go prove them; I have married a wife, I am engaged in an eager pursuit after the lust of the eye and the pride of life, and therefore cannot come." Do not fear having your name cast out as evil, or being accounted a fool for Christ's sake. Yet a little while and you shall shine like the stars in the firmament forever. Only believe, and Jesus Christ shall be to you wisdom, righteousness, sanctification, and eternal redemption. Your bodies shall be fashioned like unto His glorious body and your souls fall into all the fullness of God.

Which may God of His infinite mercy grant through Jesus Christ; to whom with You, O Holy Ghost, three persons and one God, be ascribed, as is most due, all power, might, majesty, and dominion, now and for evermore. Amen! Amen!

MARKS OF THE NEW BIRTH

by John Wesley

INTRODUCTION

The earlier dating of Whitefield's correspondence of 1740 places upon the emergence of John Wesley's doctrine of evangelical perfection makes necessary a careful review of Wesley's early sermons on the new birth. He used its text repeatedly between 1739 and 1745. In the first weeks of November, 1747, he hurriedly revised this sermon and others, including the first nine of his thirteen discourses on the Sermon on the Mount, and published them early the next year in the second volume of his *Sermons on Several Subjects*. Although we must rely upon this version of 1747, an inspection of the early sermons he had prepared for the first volume in the summer of 1746 and of his three Oxford sermons, printed as he delivered them in 1738, 1741, and 1744, indicates that the sermon below was in substance what he was preaching in 1740 and 1741, when his Sermon Register indicates he often preached from this text. I have chosen to use it because it indicates how steadfastly Wesley clung to a high doctrine of regeneration. He thought it the only foundation upon which believers might seek and find the deliverance from the remains of inbred sin that Scripture promised.

Even here, three incidental things are remarkable. One is the fact that so many of his early sermons were often on the same subjects and biblical texts that Whitefield had earlier made famous—this one in 1739. Whitefield had also published sermons on "The Almost Christian," "Satan's Devices," and "The Nature and Necessity of Self-Denial" in 1739, and "The Lord Our Righteousness" in 1741. A second is that Wesley displayed here his habit of declaring the theology of salvation in discourses jam-packed with Scripture. He and other evangelical preachers were making the Scriptures so familiar that they gained power to move even the poor and unlearned.

Third, Wesley buried in this sermon another one that he preached often, from a text he used throughout his life, Romans 14:17: "The kingdom of God is righteousness, peace, and joy in the Holy Ghost." He found that text not only a summary of what St. Paul had been saying in the Epistle to the Romans but of several other great New Testament passages, especially the opening sentences of the Sermon on the Mount and the opening paragraphs of Jesus' farewell meditation recorded in John 14 and 15. The text which provides the structure for this sermon, however, is not the one he announced but the last verse of St. Paul's famous chapter on love, I Corinthians 13.

Now for two more points that are not incidental. Wesley here spelled out in another form the point he made so clearly in 1743 in his *Earnest Appeal to Men of Reason and Religion*. Scorning merely speculative faith and the nominal Christian's trust in self-righteousness, he declared that living faith rests solely on Christ's merits and brings freedom from both the guilt and dominion of sin. This was exactly what he had said in 1738 in his "Aldersgate" sermon on *Salvation by Faith*. He repeated the point many times thereafter. Readers should beware, therefore, of attributing to the doctrine of Christian perfection the view that a holy life is the fruit of regeneration. Wesley never failed to distinguish his doctrine of entire sanctification from what he thought was the scriptural teaching that the new birth brought freedom from all such sinning as was implied in the phrase "willful transgression of a known command of God." Calvinist critics of his doctrine of heart purity labeled it "sinless perfection"; and in the sense they were using those words, Wesley denied the charge. But in the sense that he intended to convey—that is, that entire sanctification brought deliverance from the corruption within us but not from human shortcomings—the charge was true.

Finally, Wesley here displays his development of what Mildred Wynkoop has called the theology of love. He applied it to the whole sanctifying work of the Lord, which begins when God's prevening grace makes sinners aware of His infinite love, brings conviction, and enables them to trust that God will forgive and deliver them. Wesley often described the experience of regeneration by reference to Romans 5:1, which he thought declared that "the love of God is shed abroad in our hearts by the Holy Ghost" when we are born again. That same love, as all students of Wesley know, was the basis of his teaching that faith brings progress in the Christian life, that a second moment of sanctifying grace purifies the heart, and that constant growth in grace and holiness is to follow that second experience throughout one's earthly journey.

Modern believers can scarcely understand what a profound change was involved in anchoring all theology to the love God revealed to us in covenant, cross, and Comforter. For centuries the Christian religion had been geared to a "monarchical metaphor of God's relation to the world," as M. Douglas Meeks has recently pointed out. Preoccupation with God's sovereignty helped cement the false connection between monotheism and absolute monarchy. Meeks says the attributes ascribed to God in pre-Wesleyan Christian theology—that He was "one, simple, undivided, immutable, infinite, immortal, self-sufficient, and impassable"—were ones emperors needed in order "to control, to dominate, to rule an empire." John Wesley started from a different base. Partly because he saw that the God revealed in the Old Testament is love and that the command to return to loving both Him and our neighbors is central in the teaching of Moses and Isaiah, of Jesus and Paul, the Methodist founder opened a new era in theology.

By comparison with his later sermons, Wesley's description here of the fruit of the new birth leaned upon passages in the New Testament which he had since 1740 construed as dealing with entire sanctification. He spoke almost in testimony form of ministers and laymen being sealed with one "spirit of promise, the earnest of *yours* and of *our* inheritance," whereas at the conference of 1744 he declared that sealing was the fruit of being cleansed from all sin. (Indeed, by 1759 he ascribed it to a later and special gift of God to particular individuals.) He rejoiced that "the Comforter" comes to all who have faith in Christ and brings them "fulness of joy"—ideas and Scriptures that he generally used after 1740 as prooftexts of a second work of sanctifying grace. Similarly, he spoke of born-again Christians rejoicing "with joy unspeakable and full of glory" and affirmed "that we dwell in Him and He in us, because He has given us of His loving Spirit." At the beginning of the fourth section he quoted without distinction the scriptural commands "Be ye holy" and "Be ye perfect," then described the Spirit's presence as enabling the believer to be pure as Christ is pure. Finally, he exhorted the regenerate man to "let the Spirit of love and glory rest upon him, cleansing him 'from all filthiness of flesh and spirit' and teaching him to 'perfect holiness in the fear of God.'" Certainly these last words reflect the doctrine of entire sanctification. The sermon demonstrates, therefore, that Wesley often used the term "new birth" in the early years to represent his view of the whole experience of the "great salvation," including both regeneration and entire sanctification.

❖   ❖   ❖

So is everyone that is born of the Spirit (John 3:8).

1. How is everyone that is "born of the Spirit," that is, "born again," "born of God"? What is meant by the being born again, the being born of God, or being born of the Spirit? What is implied in the being a "son" or a "child of God," or having the "Spirit of adoption"? That these privileges, by the free mercy of God, are ordinarily annexed to baptism (which is thence termed by our Lord in the preceding verse the being "born of water and of the Spirit") we know; but we would know what these privileges are. What is "the new birth"?

2. Perhaps it is not needful to give a definition of this, seeing the Scripture gives none. But as the question is of the deepest concern to every child of man (since "except a man be born again," "born of the Spirit," he "cannot see the kingdom of God"), I propose to lay down the marks of it in the plainest manner, just as I find them laid down in Scripture.

I. 1. The first of these (and the foundation of all the rest) is faith. So St. Paul, "Ye are all the children of God by faith in Christ Jesus" (Gal. 3:26). So St. John, "To them gave He power" ($\dot{\varepsilon}\xi o \upsilon \sigma \iota \alpha \nu$, "right" or "privilege," it might rather be translated) "to become the sons of God, even to them that believe on His name; which were born," when they believed, "not of blood, nor of the will of the flesh," not by natural generation, "nor of the will of man," like those children adopted by men, in whom no inward change is thereby wrought, "but of God" (John 1:12, 13). And again in his general epistle, "Whosoever believes that Jesus is the Christ is born of God" (1 John 5:1).

2. But it is not a barely notional or speculative faith that is here spoken of by the apostles. It is not a bare assent to the proposition, "Jesus is the Christ," nor indeed to all the propositions contained in our creed or in the Old and New Testament. It is not merely "an assent to any or all these credible things, as credible." To say this is to say (which who could hear?) that the devils are born of God. For they have this faith. They trembling believe both that Jesus is the Christ and that all Scripture, having been given by inspiration of God, is true as God is true. It is not only "an assent to divine truth, upon the testimony of God" or "upon the evidence of miracles." For they also heard the words of His mouth and knew Him to be a faithful and true witness. They

could not but receive the testimony He gave, both of Himself and
ᶜ the Father which sent Him. They saw likewise the mighty works
⁻h He did, and thence believed that He "came forth from
ˑ Yet notwithstanding this faith they are still "reserved in
ˑf darkness until the judgment of the Great Day."
ˑr all this is no more than a dead faith. The true, living,
ˑith, which whosoever has is "born of God," is not only
ˑ act of the understanding, but a disposition which
ˑht in his heart, "a sure trust and confidence in God
ˑhe merits of Christ his sins are forgiven and he
ˑ to the favor of God." This implies that a man first
ˑe himself"; that in order to be "found in Christ," to be
ˑed through Him, he totally reject all "confidence in the
ˑ"; that "having nothing to pay," having no trust in his own
ˑorks or righteousness of any kind, he come to God as a lost,
miserable, self-destroyed, self-condemned, undone, helpless
sinner, as one whose mouth is "utterly stopped" and who is
altogether guilty before God. Such a sense of sin (commonly
called "despair" by those who speak evil of the things they know
not) together with a full conviction, such as no words can express,
that of Christ only comes our salvation and [that] an earnest
desire of that salvation must precede living faith: a trust in Him
who "for us paid our ransom by His death," and for us fulfilled the
Law in His life. This faith, then, whereby we are born of God, is
"not only a belief of all the articles of our faith, but also a true
confidence of the mercy of God, through our Lord Jesus Christ."

4. An immediate and constant fruit of this faith whereby we
are born of God, a fruit which can in no wise be separated from it,
no, not for an hour, is power over sin—power over outward sin of
every kind, over every evil word and work. For wheresoever the
blood of Christ is thus applied it "purges the conscience from
dead works." And over inward sin, for it "purifies the heart" from
every unholy desire and temper. This fruit of faith St. Paul has
largely described in the sixth chapter of his Epistle to the
Romans. "How shall we," saith he, who by faith "are dead to sin,
live any longer therein?" "Our old man is crucified with Christ,
that the body of sin might be destroyed, that henceforth we
should not serve sin." "Likewise reckon yourselves to be dead
unto sin, but alive unto God through Jesus Christ our Lord. . . . Let

not sin therefore reign," even "in your mortal body, . . . but yield yourselves unto God, as those that are alive from the dead. . . . For sin shall not have dominion over you. . . . God be thanked that you were the servants of sin, . . . but being made free"—the plain meaning is, God be thanked that though you were in the time past the servants of sin, yet now—"being free from sin you are become the servants of righteousness" (Rom. 1:6ff).

5. The same invaluable privilege of the sons of God is as strongly asserted by St. John, particularly with regard to the former branch of it, namely, power over outward sin. After he had been crying out as one astonished at the depth of the riches of the goodness of God. "Behold what manner of love the Father has bestowed upon us, that we should be called the sons of God," he says. "Beloved, now are we the sons of God. And it doth not yet appear what we shall be, but we know that when He shall appear we shall be like Him, for we shall see Him as He is" (1 John 3:1ff.). He soon adds, "Whosoever is born of God does not commit sin; for His seed remains in him, and he cannot sin because he is born of God" (1 John 3:9). But some men will say, "True, 'whosoever is born of God does not commit sin' *habitually*." *Habitually*! Whence is that? I read it not. It is not written in the Book. God plainly says, he "does not commit sin." And you add "habitually"! Who are you that mends the oracles of God, that "adds to the words of the Book"? Beware, I beseech you, lest God "add to you all the plagues that are written therein"! Especially when the comment you add is such as quite swallows up the text, so that by this $\mu\epsilon\theta o\delta\epsilon\iota\alpha \pi\lambda\alpha\nu\eta\varsigma$, this artful method of deceiving, the precious promise is utterly lost; by this $\kappa\upsilon\beta\epsilon\iota\alpha \alpha\nu\theta\rho\omega\pi\omega\nu$, this tricking and shuffling of men, the word of God is made of none effect. O beware, you that thus take from the words of this Book, that taking away the whole meaning and spirit from them leaves only what may indeed be termed a dead letter, lest God take away your part out of the Book of Life!

6. Suffer we the apostle to interpret his own words by the whole tenor of his discourse. In the fifth verse of this chapter he had said, "You know that He (Christ) was manifested to take away our sins; and in Him is no sin." What is the inference he draws from this? "Whosoever abides in Him sins not; whosoever sins has not seen Him, neither known Him" (v. 9). To his enforcement of this important doctrine he premises a highly necessary caution: "Little children, let no man deceive you" (for many will endeavor so to do, to persuade you that you may be unrighteous, that you may commit sin and yet be children of God). "He that does righteousness is righteous, even as He is righteous. He that commits sin is of the devil; for the devil sins from the beginning" (v. 7). Then follows, "Whosoever is born of God does not commit sin; for His seed remains in him, and he cannot sin, because he is born of God. In this," adds the apostle, "the children of God are manifest, and the children of the devil." By this plain mark (the committing or not committing sin) are they distinguished from each other. To the same effect are those words in his fifth chapter, "We know that whosoever is born of God sins not; but he that is begotten of God keeps himself, and that wicked one touches him not" (v. 18).

7. Another fruit of this living faith is peace. For "being justified by faith," having all our sins blotted out, "we have peace with God, through our Lord Jesus Christ" (Rom. 5:1). This indeed our Lord Himself, the night before His death, solemnly bequeathed to all His followers. "Peace," said He, "I leave with you" (you who "believe in God" and "believe also in me"), "my peace I give unto you. Not as the world gives, give I unto you. Let not your heart be troubled, neither let it be afraid" (John 14:27). And again, "These things have I spoken unto you, that in me you might have peace" (John 16:33). This is the "peace of God which passeth all understanding," that serenity of soul which it has not entered into the heart of a natural man to conceive, and which it is not possible for even the spiritual man to utter. And it is a peace which all the powers of earth and hell are unable to take from him. Waves and storms beat upon it, but they shake it not, for it is founded upon a rock. It keeps the hearts and minds of the children of God at all times and in all places. Whether they are in ease or in pain, in sickness or health, in abundance or want, they are happy in God. In every state they have learned to be content, yes, to give thanks unto God through Jesus Christ, being well assured that whatsoever is, is best, because it is His will concerning them. So that in all the vicissitudes of life their "heart stands fast, believing in the Lord."

II. 1. A second scriptural mark of those who are born of God is hope. Thus St. Peter, speaking to all the children of God who were then "scattered abroad," said, "Blessed be the God and Father of our Lord Jesus Christ, who according to His abundant mercy hath begotten us again unto a lively hope" (1 Peter 1:3; ελπιδα ζωσαν, a *lively* or *living* hope, said the apostle, because there is also a *dead* hope as well as a dead faith—a hope which is not from God but from the enemy of God and man, as evidently appears by its fruits. For as it is the offspring of pride, so it is the parent of every evil word and work.) Whereas every man that has in him this living hope is "holy as He that calls him is holy." Every man that can truly say to his brethren in Christ, " 'Beloved, now are we the sons of God, . . . and we shall see Him as He is,' " "purifies himself, even as He is pure."

2. This hope termed in the Epistle to the Hebrews πληροθυρια πιστεως (Heb. 10:22), and elsewhere πληροθυρια ελπιδος(Heb. 6:11), in our translation, the "full assurance of faith" and the "full assurance of hope," expressions the best which our language could afford, although far weaker than those in the original, [this hope,] as described in Scripture, implies, first, the testimony of our own spirit or conscience that we walk "in simplicity and godly sincerity," but, secondly and chiefly, the testimony that the Spirit of God, "bears witness with," or to, "our spirit, that we are the children of God; and if children, then heirs, heirs of God and joint-heirs with Christ."

3. Let us well observe what is here taught us by God himself touching the glorious privilege of His children. Who is it that is here said to "bear witness"? Not our spirit only, but another, even the Spirit of God. He it is who "bears witness with our spirit." What is it He bears witness of? "That we are the children of God. And if children, then heirs, heirs of God, and joint-heirs with Christ"—"if so be that we suffer with Him" (if we deny ourselves, if we take up our cross daily, if we cheerfully endure persecution or reproach for His sake) "that we may be also glorified together." And in whom does the Spirit of God bear this witness? In all who are the children of God. By this very argument does the apostle prove in the preceding verses that they are so: "As many," said he, "as are led by the Spirit of God, they are the sons of God. For you have not received the spirit of bondage again to fear; but you have received the Spirit of adoption, whereby we cry, 'Abba, Father!' " (Rom. 8:16–17). It follows, "the Spirit itself bears witness with our spirit that we are the children of God."

4. The variation of the phrase in the fifteenth verse is worthy |of| our observation. "You have received the Spirit of adoption, whereby *we* cry, "Abba, Father!' " You—as many |as| are the sons of God—have, in virtue of your sonship, received that selfsame Spirit of adoption whereby *we* cry, "Abba, Father." We, the apostles, prophets, teachers (for so the word may not improperly be understood; we, through whom you have believed, the "ministers of Christ, and stewards of the mysteries of God")— as *we* and *you* have one Lord, so we have one Spirit. As we have one faith, so have we one hope also. We and you are sealed with one "Spirit of promise," the earnest of *yours* and of *our* inheritance, the same Spirit bearing witness with yours and with our spirits "that we are the children of God."

5. And thus is the Scripture fulfilled, "Blessed are they that mourn, for they shall be comforted." For 'tis easy to believe that though sorrow may precede this witness of God's Spirit with our spirit (indeed *must* to some degree, while we groan under fear and a sense of the wrath of God abiding on us), yet as soon as any man feels it in himself his "sorrow is turned into joy." Whatsoever his pain may have been before, yet as soon as that "hour is come, he remembers the anguish no more, for joy" that he is born of God. It may be many of *you* have now sorrow, because you are "aliens from the commonwealth of Israel," because you are conscious to yourselves that you have not this Spirit, that you are "without hope and without God in the world." But when the Comforter is come, then "your heart shall rejoice," yea, "your joy shall be full"; and "that joy no man taketh from you" (John 16:22). "We joy in God," will you say, "through our Lord Jesus Christ, by whom we have now received the atonement"; "by whom we have access into this grace" (this state of grace, of favor, of reconciliation with God) "wherein we stand, and rejoice in hope of the glory of God" (Rom. 5:2). "You," St. Peter says, whom God "has begotten again unto a lively hope," "are kept by the power of God unto salvation. . . . Wherein you greatly rejoice, though now for a season, if need be, you are in heaviness through manifold temptations, that the trial of your faith . . . might be found unto praise, and honor, and glory, at the appearing of Jesus Christ, . . . in whom, though now you see Him not, you rejoice with joy unspeakable and full of glory" (1 Peter 1:5ff.).

Unspeakable indeed! It is not for the tongue of man to describe this joy in the Holy Ghost. It is "the hidden manna, . . . which no man knows saving he that receives it." But this we know, it not only remains but overflows in the depth of affliction. "Are the consolations of God small" with His children, when all earthly comforts fail? Not so. But when sufferings most abound, the consolation of His Spirit does much more abound. Insomuch that the sons of God "laugh at destruction when it comes," at want, pain, hell and the grave; as knowing Him who "has the keys of death and hell" and will shortly "cast them into the bottomless pit,"as hearing even now the "great voice out of heaven" saying, "Behold, the tabernacle of God is with men, and He will dwell with them, and they shall be His people, and God himself shall be with them and be their God. And God shall wipe away all tears from their eyes. And there shall be no more death, neither sorrow, nor crying, neither shall there be any more pain: for the former things are passed away" (Rev. 21:3–4).

III. 1. A third scriptural mark of those who are born of God, and the greatest of all, is love, even "the love of God shed abroad in their hearts by the Holy Ghost which is given unto them" (Rom. 5:5). "Because they are sons, God has sent forth the Spirit of his Son into their hearts, crying, 'Abba, Father!' " (Gal. 4:6). By this Spirit, continually looking up to God as their reconciled and loving Father, they cry to Him for their daily bread, for all things needful whether for their souls or bodies. They continually pour out their hearts before Him, knowing "they have the petitions which they ask of Him" (1 John 5:15). Their delight is in Him. He is the joy of their hearts, their "shield," and their "exceeding great reward." The desire of their soul is toward Him; it is their "meat and drink to do His will"; and they are "satisfied as with marrow and fatness, while their mouths praise Him with joyful lips" (Ps. 48:5).

2. And in this sense also "everyone that loves Him that begat loves Him that is begotten of Him" (1 John 5:1). His spirit rejoices in God his Savior. He loves the Lord Jesus Christ in sincerity. He is so "joined unto the Lord" as to be "one spirit." His soul hangs upon Him and chooses Him as altogether lovely, "the chiefest among ten thousand." He knows, he feels what that means, "My beloved is mine, and I am His" (Song of Sol. 2:16). "You are fairer than the children of men: grace is poured into your lips, because God has anointed You for ever!" (Ps. 45:2).

3. The necessary fruit of this love of God is the love of our neighbor, of every soul which God has made, not excepting our enemies, not excepting those who are now "despitefully using and persecuting us"—a love whereby we love every man *as ourselves*, as we love our own souls. Nay, our Lord has expressed it still more strongly, teaching us to "love one another even as He has loved us." Accordingly the commandment written in the hearts of all those that love God is no other than this, "As I have loved you, so love one another." Now "herein perceive we the love of God, in that He laid down His life for us. We ought," then, as the apostle justly infers, "to lay down our lives for our brethren" (1 John 3:16). If we feel ourselves ready to do this, then do we truly love our neighbor. Then "we know that we have passed from death unto life, because we" thus "love our brethren" (v. 14). "Hereby know we" that we are born of God, that we "dwell in Him, and He in us, because He has given us of His loving Spirit" (1 John 4:13). For "love is of God; and everyone that" thus "loves is born of God and knows God."

4. But some may possibly ask, "Does not the apostle say, 'This is the love of God, that we keep His commandments'?" (1 John 5:3). Yes; and this is the love of our neighbor also, in the same sense as it is the love of God. But what would you infer from hence? That the keeping the outward commandments is all that is implied in loving God with all your heart, with all your mind and soul and strength, and in loving your neighbor as yourself? That the love of God is not an affection of the soul but merely an *outward service*, and that the love of our neighbor is not a disposition of the heart but barely a course of *outward works*? To mention so wild an interpretation of the apostle's words is sufficiently to confute it. The plain indisputable meaning of that text is, "this is the" sign or proof of "the love of God," of our keeping the first and great commandment: to keep the rest of His commandments. For true love, if it be once shed abroad in our heart, will constrain us so to do, since whosoever loves God with all his heart cannot but serve Him with all his strength.

5. A second fruit then of the love of God (so far as it can be distinguished from it) is universal obedience to Him we love and conformity to His will—obedience to all the commands of God, internal and external, obedience of the heart and of the life, in every temper and in all manner of conversation. And one of the tempers most obviously implied herein is the being "zealous of good works," the hungering and thirsting to do good in every possible kind unto all men, the rejoicing to "spend and be spent for them" (for every child of man), not looking for any recompense in this world but only in the resurrection of the just.

IV. 1. Thus have I plainly laid down those marks of the new birth which I find laid down in Scripture. Thus does God Himself answer that weighty question what it is to be born of God. Such, if the appeal be made to the oracles of God, is "everyone that is born of the Spirit." This it is, in the judgment of the Spirit of God, to be a son or a child of God. It is so to *believe* in God through Christ as "not to commit sin" and to enjoy, at all times and in all places, that "peace of God which passes all understanding." It is so to *hope* in God through the Son of His love as to have not only the "testimony of a good conscience" but also the Spirit of God "bearing witness with your spirit that you are the children of God," whence cannot but spring the "rejoicing evermore in Him through whom you have received the atonement." It is so to *love* God, who has thus loved you, as you never did love any creature, so that you are constrained to love all men as yourselves, with a love not only ever burning in your hearts but flaming out in all your actions and conversations and making your whole life one "labor of love," one continued obedience to those commands, "Be merciful as your Father is merciful"; "Be holy, as I the Lord am holy"; "Be perfect, as your Father which is in heaven is perfect."

2. Who then are you that are *thus* born of God? You "know the things which are given to you of God." You well know that you are the children of God and "can assure your hearts before Him." And every one of you who has observed these words cannot but feel and know of a truth whether at this hour (answer to God and not to man!) you are thus a child of God or no. The question is not what you were made in baptism (do not evade!) but what you are now. Is the Spirit of adoption now in your heart? To your own heart let the appeal be made. I ask not whether you *were* born of water and the Spirit. But *are* you *now* the temple of the Holy Ghost which dwells in you? I allow you were "circumcised with the circumcision of Christ" (as St. Paul emphatically terms baptism). But does the Spirit of Christ and of glory *now* rest upon you? Else* "your circumcision is become uncircumcision."

3. Say not then in your heart, I *was once* baptized, therefore I *am now* a child of God. Alas, that consequence will by no means hold. How many are the baptized gluttons and drunkards, the baptized liars and common swearers, the baptized railers and evil-speakers, the baptized whoremongers, thieves, extortioners! What think you? Are these now the children of God? Verily I say unto you, whosoever you are unto whom any of the preceding characters belong, "You are of your father the devil, and the works of your father you do." Unto you I call in the name of Him whom you crucify afresh, and in His words to your circumcised predecessors, "You serpents, you generation of vipers, how can you escape the damnation of hell?"

4. How indeed, except you be born again! For you are now dead in trespasses and sins. To say then that you cannot be born again, that there is no new birth but in baptism, is to seal you all under damnation, to consign you to hell, without help, without hope. And perhaps some may think this just and right. In their zeal for the Lord of Hosts they may say, "Yes, cut off the sinners, the Amalekites! Let these Gibeonites be utterly destroyed! They deserve no less." No, nor I, nor you; mine and your desert, as well as theirs, is hell. And it is mere mercy, free undeserved mercy, that *we* are not now in unquenchable fire. You will say, "But we are washed, we were born again of water and of the Spirit." So *were* they. This therefore hinders not at all, but that you may *now* be even as they. Know you not that "what is highly esteemed of men is an abomination in the sight of God"? Come forth, you "saints of

---

*Meaning "otherwise."

the world," you that are honored of men, and see who will cast the first stone at them, at these wretches not fit to live upon the earth, these common harlots, adulterers, murderers. Only learn first what that means: "Whosoever hates his brother is a murderer" (1 John 3:15); "Whosoever looks on a woman to lust after her has committed adultery with her already in his heart" (Matt. 5:28); "You adulterers and adulteresses, know you not that the friendship of the world is enmity with God?" (James 4:4).

5. "Verily, verily, I say unto you, you" also "must be born again." "Except you be born again, you cannot see the kingdom of God." Lean no more on the staff of that broken reed, that you *were* born again in baptism. Who denies that you were then made "children of God, and heirs of the kingdom of heaven"? But notwithstanding this, you are now children of the Devil; therefore you must be born again. And let not Satan put it into your heart to cavil at a word, when the thing is clear. You have heard what are the marks of the children of God. All you who have them not on your souls, baptized or unbaptized, must needs receive them, or without doubt you will perish everlastingly. And if you have been baptized, your only hope is this: that those who were made the children of God by baptism, but are now the children of the Devil, may yet again receive "power to become the sons of God"; that they may receive again what they have lost, even the "Spirit of adoption, crying in their hearts, 'Abba, Father!' "

6. Amen, Lord Jesus! May every one who prepares his heart yet again to seek your face receive again that Spirit of adoption and cry out, Abba, Father! Let him now again have power [so] to believe in your name as to become a child of God, as to know and feel he has "redemption in your blood, even the forgiveness of sins" and that he "cannot commit sin, because he is born of God." Let him be now "begotten again unto a living hope," so as to "purify himself, as You are pure!" And "because he is a son," let the Spirit of love and of glory rest upon him, cleansing him "from all filthiness of flesh and spirit" and teaching him to "perfect holiness in the fear of God"!

CHRIST, THE BELIEVER'S WISDOM, RIGHTEOUSNESS, SANCTIFICATION, AND REDEMPTION

by George Whitefield

INTRODUCTION

Readers will be interested to compare this sermon with two others, one by Whitefield and one by John Wesley, on the same text (Jeremiah 23:6) and subject ("The Lord Our Righteousness"), but written twenty-five years apart. Just as Whitefield was careful in that sermon and in the one published here to rebuke those who used the doctrine of imputed righteousness to excuse wrongdoing, Wesley criticized those who thought Christ's imparted righteousness excused them from relying on His Atonement to cover their unwitting sins and all the evil that flowed from their imperfect judgment or their mental and bodily frailty.

Those who, from Charles Finney to historian William McLaughlin, have wondered how a believer in predestination and the final perseverance of the saints can combine those doctrines with an effective evangelistic appeal may see the answer in this sermon. In several passages of it, Whitefield explicitly linked evangelism to Calvinism. Published in Edinburgh in 1742 and soon after in other cities in England and America, it illustrates the growing attachment of the evangelist to Reformed doctrines. He wrote it early in 1741, aboard ship on his way home from Georgia, but had preached it in various forms, he tells us, during the preceding months. It displays, therefore, Whitefield's stout resistance by that time to John Wesley's teaching about purity of heart.

The sermon also shows, however, that anyone who has claimed to be a follower of John Calvin but has stressed grace so much as to minimize obedience to the law of righteousness has greatly erred. Not only was Calvin very clear on the point, but so also were the English Puritans who, on the eve of Oliver Cromwell's revolution, adopted the "covenant theology" of the Westminster Confession of Faith. A hundred years later, the devotion of the Presbyterian and Congregational clergy of Scotland and America to the conviction that Christians who are born again must live holy lives persuaded Whitefield that they could be his spiritual teachers. They soon became more influential upon him than John and Charles Wesley. They, like the young Whitefield, insisted as strongly as any Wesleyan ever did on deliverance from the dominion, though not from the being, of inbred sin.

By the time he printed this sermon, however, Whitefield had backed away somewhat from the emphasis of his earlier preaching on a holy life. His withdrawal did not stem from Wesley's idea that regeneration brought ethical transformation, but from the older man's belief, reached in the fall of 1739, that the Bible set forth a second inward experience properly called *entire* sanctification, which promised to destroy the "original" impulse to sin in the human heart. Both men always taught that the dominion of this inward corruption over thought and action was broken when one was born again. This remained, until about one hundred years ago, a central affirmation of all evangelical revivalists, whether Puritans, Pietists, or peace-church people, or those who followed Wesley as Anglican evangelicals or Methodists. But Whitefield and other Calvinists stoutly resisted the doctrine of cleansing from inward corruption.

Although Wesley always affirmed the doctrine of free grace, he never included in his editions of his collected works his early sermon of April, 1739, on that question. That sermon offended Whitefield when Wesley first preached it in Bristol and even more when he published it the preceding winter. It did not appear under Wesleyan auspices again until Joseph Benson resurrected it in the edition of Wesley's *Works* he published in 1809–13. Indeed, before Whitefield's death and the ensuing "Calvinistic controversy," Wesley rarely preached against unconditional election. But he did publish several brief works against it in the preceding years, notably *Predestination Calmly Considered* in 1752; and he often spoke against the doctrine in the annual conferences of Methodist preachers. He also wrote against it in many passages of his *Explanatory Notes* on the Old and New Testaments. Moreover, he and his brother Charles wrote many hymns that celebrated the promise to all persons of saving grace.

Finally, one can see here the evangelical style of finding an outline of a sermon in the words of its scriptural text, and the early maturing of Whitefield's use of that style. None of his language smacks of an Oxford education. He had learned already what Wesley wished for, the ability to speak plain words to plain people; usually Whitefield relied on words of one or two syllables. The power and biblical integrity of his appeal in the latter portion of the sermon will be as evident to modern readers as it was to his hearers long ago.

❖   ❖   ❖

But of him are ye in Christ Jesus, who of God is made unto us wisdom, righteousness, sanctification, and redemption (1 Cor. 1:30).

Of all the verses in the Book of God, this which I have now read to you is, I believe, one of the most comprehensive. What glad tidings does it bring to believers! What precious privileges are they herein invested with! How are they here led to the fountain of them all, I mean the love, the everlasting love of God the Father of whom are you in Christ Jesus, "who of God is made unto us wisdom, righteousness, sanctification, and redemption."

Without referring you at present to the context, I shall from these words,

First, point out to you the fountain from which all those blessings flow, which the elect of God partake of in Jesus Christ, "who of God is made unto us...."

Secondly, I shall consider what those blessings are, namely, "wisdom, righteousness, sanctification, and redemption."

And, *first,* I would point out to you, the fountain from which all those blessings flow, which the elect of God partake of in Jesus, "who of God is made unto us," that is, God the Father, for He it is that is spoken of here. Not as tho' Jesus Christ was not God as well as He. But God the Father is the fountain of the deity, and if we consider Jesus Christ acting as mediator, God the Father is greater than He. There was an eternal contract between the Father and the Son. "I have made," says God, "a covenant with my chosen, and I have sworn unto David my servant" (which David was a type of Christ, with whom the Father made a covenant), that if He would obey and suffer and make himself a sacrifice for sin, He should "see His seed, He should prolong his days, and the pleasure of the Lord should prosper in His hands." This compact our Lord refers to in that glorious prayer recorded in the seventeenth chapter of St. John; and therefore He prays for, or rather demands with a full assurance, all that were given to Him by the Father.

"Father," says He, "I will that they also whom You have given me be with me where I am." For this same reason the apostle breaks out into praising God, even the Father of our Lord Jesus Christ. For He loved the elect with an everlasting love, or, as our Lord expresses it, "before the foundation of the world." And therefore, to show them to what they were beholden for their salvation, our Lord, in the twenty-fifth [chapter] of Matthew, represents himself saying, "Come, you blessed children of My Father, receive the kingdom prepared for you from the foundation of the world." And thus in reply to the mother of Zebedee's children, He says, "It is not mine to give, but it shall be given to them for whom it is prepared of the Father." The apostle, therefore, when here speaking of the Christian's privileges, lest they should sacrifice to their own drag* or think their salvation was owing to their own faithfulness or improvement of their own free will, reminds them to look back on the everlasting love of God the Father, "who of God is made unto us," and so on.

Would to God this point of doctrine was considered more, and people were more studious of the covenant of redemption between the Father and the Son. We should then not have so much disputing against the doctrine of election or hear it condemned (even by good men) as a doctrine of devils. For my own part, I cannot see how true humbleness of mind can be attained without a knowledge of it. And tho' I will not say that every one who denies election is a bad man, yet I will say, with that sweet singer Mr. Trail, it is a very bad sign. Such a one, whoever he be, I think can not know himself. For if we deny election we must (say what we will) partly at least glory in ourselves for suffering Christ to redeem and save us. But our redemption is so ordered that no flesh should glory in the divine presence. And hence it is that the pride of man opposes this doctrine, because according to this doctrine, and no other, "He that glories must glory only in the Lord." But what shall I say? Election is a mystery that shines with such resplendent brightness that, to make use of the words of one who has drank deeply of electing love, it dazzles the weak eyes even of some of

---

*Meaning "pull" or "influence."

God's dear children. However, tho' they know it not, all the blessings they receive, all the privileges they do or will enjoy thro' Jesus Christ, flow from the everlasting love of God the Father. "But of Him are you in Christ Jesus, who of God is made unto us wisdom, righteousness, sanctification, and redemption."

What these blessings are, which are here through Christ made over to the elect, I come in the *next* place to consider.

And first, Christ is made to them *wisdom*. But wherein does true wisdom consist? Were I to ask some of you, perhaps you would say, in indulging the lust of the flesh and saying to your souls, "eat, drink, and be merry." But this is only the wisdom of brutes. They have as good a gust and relish for sensual pleasures as the greatest epicure on the earth. Others would tell me true wisdom consisted in adding house to house and field to field, and calling lands after their own names. But this cannot be true wisdom, for riches often take themselves wings and fly away, like an eagle towards heaven. Even wisdom itself assures us that "a man's life does not consist in the abundance of the things which he possesses." Vanity, vanity, all these things are vanity. For if riches leave not the owner, the owners must soon leave them; "for rich men must also die, and leave their riches for others." Their riches cannot procure them a redemption from the grave, whither we are all hastening apace. But perhaps you despise riches and pleasure and therefore place wisdom in the knowledge of books. But it is possible for you to tell the numbers of the stars and call them all by their names, and yet be mere fools. Learned men are not always wise. Nay, our common learning, so much cried up, makes men only so many accomplished fools.

To keep you therefore no longer in suspense, and withal to humble you, I will send you to an heathen to school, to learn what true wisdom is. "Know thyself," was a saying of one of the wise men of Greece. This is certainly true wisdom, and this is that wisdom spoken of in the text and which Jesus Christ is made to all elect sinners. They are made to know themselves so as not to think more highly of themselves than they ought to think. Before they were darkness, now they are light in the Lord; and in that light they see their own darkness. They now bewail that they are fallen creatures by nature, dead in trespasses and sins, sons and heirs of hell, and children of wrath. They now see that all their righteousnesses are but as filthy rags, that there is no health in their souls, that they are poor and miserable, blind and naked, and that there is no name given under heaven whereby they can be saved but that of Jesus Christ. They see the necessity of closing with a Savior, and the wisdom of God in appointing Him to be a Savior. They are also made willing to accept of salvation upon our Lord's own terms and to receive Him as their all in all. Thus Christ is made to them "wisdom."

Secondly, *righteousness* —"who of God is made unto us, wisdom, righteousness"—that is, Christ's whole personal righteousness is made over to and accounted theirs. Being enabled to lay hold on Christ by faith, God the Father blots out their transgressions as with a thick cloud, their sins, their iniquities, He remembers no more. They are made the righteousness of God in Christ Jesus, who is the end of the law for righteousness to every one that believes. In one sense, now God sees no sin in them. The whole covenant of works is fulfilled in them. They are actually justified, acquitted, and looked upon as righteous in the sight of God. They are perfectly accepted in the beloved, they are complete in Him. The flaming sword of God's wrath which before moved every way is now removed and free access given to the tree of life. They are enabled now to reach out the arm of faith and pluck, and live for evermore. Hence it is that the apostle, under a sense of this blessed privilege, breaks out into this triumphant language: "It is Christ that justifies, who is he that condemns me?" Does sin condemn? Christ's righteousness delivers believers from the guilt of it. Christ is their "Jesus," their Savior, and is become a propitiation for their sins. Who therefore shall lay any thing to the charge of God's elect? Does the law condemn? By having Christ's righteousness imputed to them, they are dead to the law, as a covenant of works. Christ has fulfilled it for them and in their stead. Does death threaten them? They need not fear. The sting of death is sin, the strength of sin is the law; but God has given them victory by imputing to them the righteousness of the Lord Jesus.

And what a privilege is here! Well might the angels at the birth of Christ say to the humble shepherds, "Behold I bring you glad tidings of great joy." For unto you that believe in Christ, a Savior is born. And well may they rejoice at the conversion of poor sinners, for the Lord is their righteousness. They have peace with God, through faith in Christ's blood, and shall never enter into condemnation. O believers (for this discourse is intended in a special manner for you), lift up your heads, "rejoice in the Lord always, again I say rejoice." Christ is made to you of God, righteousness. What then should you fear? You are made the righteousness of God in Him. You may be* called "the Lord our righteousness." Of what then should you be afraid? What shall separate you henceforward from the love of Christ? Shall tribulation, or distress, or persecution, or famine, or nakedness, or peril, or sword? No, I am persuaded that neither death, nor life, nor angels, nor principalities, nor powers, nor things present, nor things to come, nor height, nor depth, nor any other creature shall be able to separate you from the love of God, which is in Christ Jesus our Lord, who of God is made unto you righteousness.

This is a glorious privilege, but this is only the beginning of the happiness of believers. Christ is not only made to them righteousness but *sanctification*. By sanctification, I do not mean a bare hypocritical attendance on outward ordinances (tho' rightly-informed Christians will think it their duty and privilege constant-ly to attend on all outward ordinances). Nor do I mean by sanctification a bare outward reformation and a few transient convictions or a little legal sorrow; for all this an unsanctified man may have. But by sanctification I mean a total renovation of the whole man. By the righteousness of Christ, believers become legally, by sanctification they are made spiritually alive. By one they are entitled to, by the other made meet for glory. They are sanctified therefore throughout, in spirit, soul, and body.

Their understandings, which were before dark, now become light in the Lord, and their wills, before contrary to, now become one with the will of God. Their affections are now set on things above. Their memory is now filled with divine things. Their natural consciences are now enlightened. Their members, which were before instruments of uncleanness and of iniquity unto iniquity, are now instruments of righteousness and true holiness. In short, they are new creatures. Old things are passed away, all

---

*In his later edition of Twenty-Three Sermons, in 1745, Whitefield made the preceding three words read, "who now is," without beginning a new sentence.

things are become new in their hearts. Sin has now no longer dominion over them. They are freed from the power, tho' not the indwelling and being of it. They are holy both in heart and life, even in all manner of conversation. They are made partakers of a divine nature. . . . From Jesus Christ they receive grace for grace; and every grace that is in Christ is copied and transcribed into their souls. They are transformed into His likeness; He is formed within them; they dwell in Him, and He in them. They are led by and bring forth the fruits of His Spirit. They know that Christ is their "Emmanuel," God with and in them. They are living temples of the Holy Ghost. And therefore being a holy habitation unto the Lord, the whole Trinity dwells and walks in them. Even here, they sit together with Christ in heavenly places and are vitally united to Him, their head, by a living faith. Their redeemer, their maker, is their husband. They are flesh of His flesh, bone of His bone. They talk, they walk with Him as a man talks and walks with his friend. In short, they are one with Christ, even as Jesus Christ and the Father are one.

Thus is Christ made to believers sanctification. And O what a privilege is this: to be changed from beasts into saints, from a devilish into a divine nature, to be thus translated from the kingdom of Satan into the kingdom of God's dear Son! To put off the old man which is corrupt and thus to put on the new man, which is created after God in righteousness and true holiness—O, what an unspeakable blessing is this! I almost stand amazed at the contemplation of it. Well might the apostle exhort believers to rejoice in the Lord. Indeed they have reason always to rejoice, yes, to rejoice in their beds, for the kingdom of God is in them. They are changed from glory to glory, even by the Spirit of the Lord. Well may this be a mystery to the natural, for it is a mystery even to the spiritual man himself, a mystery which he cannot fathom. Does it not often dazzle your eyes, O you children of God, to look at your own brightness, when the candle of the Lord shines out and your redeemer lifts up the light of His blessed countenance upon your souls? Are not you astonished when you feel the love of God shed abroad in your hearts abundantly by the Holy Ghost, and God holds out the golden scepter of His mercy and bids you ask what you will and it shall be given you? Does not that peace of God, which keeps and rules your hearts, surpass the utmost limits of your understandings? And is not the joy you feel unspeakable? Is it not full of glory? I am persuaded it is. And in your secret communion, when the Lord glows in upon your souls, you are as it were swallowed up in, or, to use the apostle's phrase, "filled with all the fulness of God." Are not you ready to cry out with Solomon, "And will the Lord indeed dwell thus with men? How is it that we should be thus thy sons and daughters, O Lord Almighty!"

If you are children of God and know what it is to have fellowship with the Father and the Son, if you walk by faith and not by sight, I am assured this is frequently the language of your hearts.

But look forward and see an unbounded prospect of eternal happiness lying before you, O believer! What you have already received are only the first fruits, like the cluster of grapes brought out of the land of Canaan—only an earnest and pledge of yet infinitely better things to come. The harvest is yet to follow. Your grace is hereafter to be swallowed up in glory. Your great Joshua, your great high priest, shall administer an abundant entrance unto you into the land of promise, that rest which awaits the children of God. For Christ is not only made to believers wisdom, righteousness, and sanctification, but also *redemption*.

But before we enter upon the explanation and contemplation of this privilege, from what has been said we may first learn the great mistake of Archbishop Tillotson and writers of his stamp, who, notwithstanding they talk of sanctification and inward holiness (as indeed sometimes they do, tho' in a very loose and superficial manner), yet they generally make it the *cause*, whereas they should consider it as the *effect* of our justification. Of whom "are you in Christ Jesus, who of God is made unto us wisdom, righteousness," and then "sanctification." For Christ's righteousness, or that which Christ has done in our stead without us, is the sole cause of our acceptance in the sight of God, and of all holiness wrought in us. To this, and not to the light within or any thing wrought within, should poor sinners seek for justification in the sight of God. For the sake of Christ's righteousness alone, and not any thing wrought in us, does God look favorably upon us.

Our sanctification at best in this life is not complete. Tho' we are delivered from the power we are not freed from the inbeing of sin. But not only the dominion but the inbeing of sin is forbidden by the perfect law of God. For it is not said, "You shall not give way to lust," but "You shall not lust." So that while the principle of lust remains in the least degree in our hearts, tho' we are otherwise ever so holy, yet we cannot, on account of that, hope for acceptance with God. We must first, therefore, look for a righteousness without us, even the righteousness of our Lord Jesus Christ. For this reason the apostle mentions it and puts it before sanctification in the words of the text. And whosoever teaches any other doctrine does not preach the truth as it is in Jesus.

Secondly, from hence also the antinomians and formal hypocrites may be confuted, who talk of Christ without but know nothing experimentally of a work of sanctification wrought within them. Whatever they may pretend to, since Christ is not in them the Lord is not their righteousness, and they have no well grounded hope of glory. For tho' sanctification is not the cause, yet it is the effect of our acceptance with God; "who of God is made unto us righteousness, and sanctification." He therefore that is really in Christ is a new creature. It's not going back to a covenant of works to look into our hearts and, seeing that they are changed and renewed, from thence form[ing] a comfortable and well-grounded assurance of the safety of our states. No, this is what we are directed to in Scripture: by bringing forth the fruits, we are to judge whether or no we ever did truly partake of the Spirit of God. "We know," says John, "that we are passed from death unto life, because we love the brethren." And however we may talk of Christ's righteousness and exclaim against legal preachers, yet if we are not holy in heart and life, if we are not sanctified and renewed by the Spirit in our minds, we are self-deceivers, we are only formal hypocrites. For we must not put asunder what God has joined together. We must keep the medium between the two extremes—not insist so much on the one hand upon Christ without as to exclude Christ within, as an evidence of our being His and as a preparation for future happiness, nor on the other hand, so depend on inherent righteousness or holiness wrought in us as to exclude the righteousness of Jesus Christ without us.

But let us go on and take a view of the other link, or rather the end of the believer's golden chain of privileges. But we must look very high, for the very top of it, like Jacob's ladder, reaches heaven where all believers will be drawn up and placed at the right hand of God. "Who of God is made unto us wisdom, righteousness, sanctification, and *redemption.*"

This is a golden chain indeed! And what is best of all, not one link can ever be broken asunder from another. And were there no other text in the Book of God, this single one sufficiently proves the final perseverance of true believers. For never did God yet justify a man whom He did not sanctify, nor sanctify one whom He did not completely redeem and glorify. No, as for God, His way, His work is perfect; He always carried on and finished the work He began. Thus it was in the first, so it is in the new creation. When God says, "Let there be light," there is light that shines more and more unto the perfect day, when believers enter into their eternal rest as God entered into His. Those whom God has justified, He has in effect glorified. For as a man's worthiness was not the cause of God's giving him Christ's righteousness, so neither shall his unworthiness be a cause of His taking it away. God's gifts and callings are without repentance. And I cannot think they are clear in the notion of Christ's righteousness who deny the final perseverance of the saints. I fear they understand justification in that low sense which I understood it in a few years ago, as implying no more than remission of sins. But it not only signifies remission of sins past, but also a *federal right* to all good things to come. If God has given us His only Son, how shall He not with Him freely give us all things? Therefore, the apostle, after he says, "who of God is made unto us righteousness," does not say, "perhaps He *may* be" made to us sanctification and redemption, but He "*is* made." For there is an eternal, indissoluble connection between these blessed privileges. As the obedience of Christ is imputed to believers, so His perseverance in that obedience is to be imputed to them also. And it argues great ignorance of the covenant of grace and redemption to object against it.

But to return, by the word redemption we are to understand not only a complete delivery from all evil but also a full enjoyment of all good, both in body and soul. I say both in body and soul, for the Lord is for the body. The bodies of the saints in this life are temples of the Holy Ghost. God makes a covenant with the dust of believers. After death, tho' worms destroy them, yet even in their flesh shall they hereafter see God. I fear indeed there are some Sadducees in our days, or at least heretics, who say either that there is no resurrection of the body or that the resurrection is past already, namely in our regeneration. Hence it is that our Lord's coming in the flesh at the Day of Judgment, is denied, and consequently we throw aside the sacrament of the Lord's Supper. For why should we remember the Lord's death till He comes to judgment, when He is already come to judge our hearts and will not come a second time? But all this is only the reasoning of unlearned, unstable men, who certainly know not what they say nor whereof they affirm. That we must follow our Lord in . . . regeneration and be partakers of a new birth, that Christ must come into our hearts, we freely confess; and we hope when speaking of those things we speak no more than what we know and feel. But then it is plain that Jesus Christ will come hereafter to judgment, and that He ascended into heaven with the body which He had here on earth. For, says He, after His resurrection, "Handle me, and see, a spirit has not flesh and bones, as you see me have." And it is plain that Christ's resurrection was an earnest of ours. For, says the apostle, "Christ is risen from the dead, and become the first fruits of them that sleep." And as in Adam all die and are subject to mortality, so all that are in Christ, the second Adam, who represented believers as their federal head, shall certainly be made alive, that is, rise again with their bodies at the last day.

Here then, O believers, is one, tho' the lowest, degree of that redemption which you are to be partakers of hereafter. I mean the redemption of your bodies. For this corruptible must put on incorruption, this mortal must put on immortality. Your bodies as well as souls were given to Jesus Christ by the Father. They have been companions in watching and fasting and praying. Your bodies, therefore, as well as souls, shall Jesus Christ raise up at the last day. Fear not, therefore, O believers, to look into the grave. For to you it is no other than a consecrated dormitory, where your bodies shall sleep quietly till the morning of the resurrection. When the voice of the archangel shall sound and the trump of God give the general alarm, "Arise you dead, and come to judgment," earth, air, fire, [and] water shall give up your scattered atoms, and both in body and soul shall you be ever with the Lord.

I doubt not but many of you are groaning under crazy carcasses, and complain often that the mortal body weighs down the immortal soul; at least this is my case. But let us have a little patience, and we shall be delivered from our earthly prisons. Ere it be long these tabernacles of clay shall be dissolved and we shall be clothed with our house which is from heaven. Hereafter our bodies shall be spiritualized and shall be so far from hindering our souls through weakness that they shall become strong—so strong as to bear up under an exceeding and eternal weight of glory. Others again may have deformed bodies, emaciated with sickness and worn out with labor and age. But wait a little till your blessed change by death comes. Then your bodies shall be renewed and made glorious, like unto Christ's glorious body; of which we may form some faint idea from the account given us of our Lord's transfiguration on the mount when, it is said, "His raiment became bright and glistening, and His face brighter than the sun." Well then may a believer break out into the apostle's triumphant language, "O death, where is thy sting! O grave, where is thy victory!"

But what is the redemption of the body, in comparison of the redemption of the better part, our souls? I must therefore say to you believers, as the angel said to John, come up higher, and let us take as clear a view as we can at such a distance of the redemption Christ has purchased for you, and will shortly put you in actual possession of. Already you are justified, already you are sanctified, and thereby freed from the guilt and dominion of sin. But, as I observed before, the being and indwelling of sin yet remains in you. God sees it proper to leave some Amalekites in the land, to keep his Israel in action. The most perfect Christian, I am persuaded, must agree according to one of our articles, "that the corruption of nature remains even in the regenerate; that the flesh lusts always against the spirit, and the spirit against the flesh." So that believers cannot do things for God with that perfection they desire. This grieves their righteous souls day by day, and with the holy apostle makes them cry out, "Who shall deliver us from the body of this death!" I thank God our Lord Jesus Christ, but not completely before the day of our dissolution.

Then will the very being of sin be destroyed and an eternal stop put to inbred, indwelling corruption.

And is not this a great redemption? I am sure believers esteem it so. For there is nothing grieves the heart of a child of God so much as the remains of indwelling sin. Again, believers are often in heaviness through manifold temptations. God sees that it is needful and good for them so to be. And tho' they may be highly favored and wrapped up in communion with God, even to the third heaven, yet a messenger of Satan is often sent to buffet them, lest they should be puffed up with the abundance of revelations. But be not weary, be not faint in your minds; the time of your complete redemption draws nigh. In heaven the wicked one shall cease from troubling you and your weary souls shall enjoy an everlasting rest; his fiery darts cannot reach those blissful regions. Satan will never come any more to appear with, disturb, or accuse the sons of God, when once the Lord Jesus Christ shuts the door. Your righteous souls are now grieved, day by day, at the ungodly conversation of the wicked. Tares now grow up among the wheat; wolves come in sheep's clothing. But the redemption spoken of in the text will free your souls from all anxiety on these accounts. Hereafter you shall enjoy a perfect communion of saints; nothing that is unholy or unsanctified shall enter into the Holy of Holies which is prepared for you above. This, and all manner of evil whatsoever, you shall be delivered from when your redemption is hereafter made complete in heaven. Not only so, but you shall enter into the full enjoyment of all good. It is true, all saints will not have the same degree of happiness, but all will be as happy as their hearts can hold. Believers, you shall judge evil, and familiarly converse with good angels. You shall sit down with Abraham, Isaac, Jacob, and all the spirits of just men made perfect. And to sum up all your happiness in one word, you shall see God the Father, Son, and Holy Ghost, and by seeing God be more and more like Him, and pass from glory to glory, even to all eternity.

But I must stop; the glories of the upper world crowd in so fast upon my soul that I am lost in the contemplation of them. Brethren, the redemption spoken of is unutterable; we cannot here find it out. Eye has not seen, nor ear heard, nor has it entered into the hearts of the most holy men living to conceive how great it is. Were I to entertain you whole ages with an account of it, when you come to heaven you must say with [the Queen of] Sheba, "Not half, no, not the thousandth part was told us." All we can do here is to go up on Mount Pisgah and by the eye of faith take a distant view of the promised land. We may see it, as Abraham did Christ, afar off and rejoice in it; but here we only know in part. Blessed be God, there is a time coming when we shall know God, even as we are known, and God be all in all. "Lord Jesus, accomplish the number of thine elect. Lord Jesus, hasten thy kingdom."

And now, where are the scoffers of these last days, who count the lives of Christians madness and their end to be without honor? Unhappy men, you know not what you do. Were your eyes open and had you senses to discern spiritual things, you would not speak all manner of evil against the children of God, but you would esteem them as the excellent ones of the earth and envy their happiness. Your souls would hunger and thirst after it. You also would become fools for Christ's sake. You boast of wisdom; so did the philosophers of Corinth. But your wisdom is the foolishness of folly in the sight of God. What will your wisdom avail you if it does not make you wise unto salvation? Can you, with all your wisdom, propose a more consistent scheme to build your hopes of salvation on than what has been now laid down before you? Can you, with all the strength of natural reason, find out a better way of acceptance with God than by the righteousness of the Lord Jesus Christ? Is it right to think your own works can in any measure deserve or procure it? If not, why will you not believe in Him? Why will you not submit to His righteousness? Can you deny that you are fallen creatures? Do not you find that you are full of disorders and that these disorders make you unhappy? Do not you find that you cannot change your own hearts? Have you not resolved many and many a time, and have not your corruptions yet dominion over you? Are you not bond slaves to your lusts and led captive by the Devil at his will? Why then will you not come to Christ for sanctification?

Do you not desire to die the death of the righteous, . . . that your future state may be like theirs? I am persuaded you cannot bear the thoughts of being annihilated, much less of being miserable for ever. Whatever you may pretend, if you speak truth you must confess that conscience breaks in upon you in your more sober intervals, whether you will or not, and even constrains you to believe that hell is no painted fire. And why then will you not come to Christ? He alone can procure you everlasting redemption. Haste, haste away to Him, poor beguiled sinners. You lack wisdom. Ask it of Christ; who knows but He may give it you? He is able. For He is the wisdom of the Father; He is that wisdom which was from everlasting. You have no righteousness. Away to Christ; He is the end of the law for righteousness to every one that believes. You are unholy. Flee to the Lord Jesus; He is full of grace and truth, and of His fulness all may receive that believe in Him. You are afraid to die. Let this drive you to Christ; He has the keys of death and hell. In Him is plenteous redemption. He alone can open the door which leads to everlasting life.

Let not therefore the deceived reasoner boast any longer of his pretended reason. Whatever you may think, it is the most unreasonable thing in the world not to believe on Jesus Christ, whom God hath sent. Why, why will you die? Why will you not come unto Him, that you may have life? Ho, every one that thirsts, come unto the waters of life and drink freely; come, buy, without money and without price. Were these blessed privileges in the text to be purchased by money, you might say we are poor and cannot buy. Or were they to be conferred only on sinners of such a rank or degree, then you might say, how can such sinners as we expect to be so highly favored? But they are to be freely given of God to the worst of sinners—to us, says the apostle, to me a persecutor, to you Corinthians, who were unclean, drunkards, covetous persons, idolaters. Therefore each poor sinner may say then, why not unto me? Has Christ but one blessing? What if He has blessed millions by turning them away from their iniquities; yet He still continues the same. He lives for ever to make intercession, and therefore will bless you, even you also, tho' like Esau, you have been profane and hitherto despised your heavenly Father's birthright. Even now, if you believe, Christ will be made to you of God wisdom, righteousness, sanctification, and redemption.

But I must turn again to believers, for whose instruction, as I observed before, this discourse was particularly intended. You see, brethren, partakers of the heavenly calling, what great blessings are treasured up for you in Jesus Christ your head, and what you are entitled to by believing on His name. Take heed therefore that you walk worthy of the vocation wherewith you are called. Think often how highly you are favored, and remember you have not chosen Christ but Christ has chosen you. Put on (as the elect of God) humbleness of mind, and glory; but O, let it be only in the Lord. For you have nothing but what you have received of God. By nature you were as foolish, as legal, as unholy, and in as damnable a condition as others. Be pitiful, therefore, be courteous; and as sanctification is a progressive work, beware of thinking you have already attained. Let him that is holy be holy still, knowing that he who is most pure in heart shall hereafter enjoy the clearest vision of God. Let indwelling sin be your daily burden, and not only bewail and lament but see that you subdue it daily by the power of divine grace; and look up to Jesus continually to be the finisher as well as author of your faith. Build not on your own faithfulness but on God's unchangeableness. Take heed of thinking you stand by the power of your own free will. The everlasting love of God the Father must be your only hope and consolation. Let this support you under all trials. Remember that God's gifts and calling are without repentance, that Christ having once loved you will love you to the end. Let this constrain you to obedience and make you long and look for that blessed time when He shall not only be your *wisdom*, and *righteousness*, and *sanctification*, but also complete and everlasting *redemption*.

Glory be to God in the highest.

AN EARNEST APPEAL TO MEN OF REASON AND RELIGION

by John Wesley

INTRODUCTION

In the fall of 1743, John Wesley wrote a famous appeal to thoughtful clergymen and lay people in the Church of England, and to the scholarly world generally. He implored his readers to think through the Wesleyan idea of salvation. The first and last portions of that *Earnest Appeal* appear below. It was written five years after Aldersgate Street and four years after Wesley had begun to see the promise of perfect love as a second crucial "moment" in the process by which God designed to renew His children in righteousness and love.

The writing is plain enough, even when Wesley quotes long-forgotten hymns and literary passages. His primary concern is the centrality of grace and faith to the enjoyment of salvation and to growth in holiness throughout the Christian life. His accustomed use of the idea of "spiritual senses" is spelled out here in a description of faith as the eye, the ear, the palate or taste, and the feeling of the soul. Then, without ever mentioning the formal theological term "prevenient grace," Wesley emphasized in several passages the scriptural points that faith is the "free gift" of God and that the consciousness of pardoning mercy is the ground of righteous behavior. Toward the end he inserts a powerful short paragraph on the limits and promise of Christian perfection.

Wesley's long closing exhortation is based upon both Scripture and the longings of the human heart. It is blunt enough to suit any earnest evangelist, yet loving enough for all who, like Wesley, think that kindliness is the secret to persuading men and women to believe. Woven into the exhortation is a continuing rational and biblical defense of the Methodist teaching that the new birth gives victory over "committing sin" and that Christian perfection is loving God "with all our heart and serving Him with all our strength." Both experiences are grounded on faith, however—defined here as a "trust and confidence" in "the love of God to our souls."

It is difficult to understand why the conference of Methodist preachers, which met for the first time the next year, thought John Wesley should enlarge upon this treatise. But in response to their suggestion he issued two years later his *Farther Appeal*, addressed primarily to clergymen and theologians and grounded much more extensively upon the teachings and traditions of the Church of England. Its closing sections were long exhortations to thoughtful believers in a variety of Christian sects. Both these essays and other related ones were edited from Wesley's revised texts by Frank Baker and used by Gerald Cragg in the eleventh volume of the Oxford edition of *The Works of John Wesley*, now appearing at the Abingdon Press as the Bicentennial edition. But the text used below is from the second edition, which appeared at Bristol almost simultaneously with the first London edition in 1743.

❖   ❖   ❖

1. Although it is with us "a very small thing to be judged of you or of man's judgment," seeing we know God will make our innocence "as clear as the light, and our just dealing as the noonday," yet are we ready to give any that are willing to hear a plain account both of our principles and actions, as having "renounced the hidden things of shame" and desiring nothing more than "by manifestation of the truth to commend ourselves to every man's conscience in the sight of God."

2. We see—and who does not?—the numberless follies and miseries of our fellow creatures. We see on every side either men of no religion at all or men of a lifeless, formal religion. We are grieved at the sight and should greatly rejoice if by any means we might convince some that there is a better religion to be attained, a religion worthy of God that gave it. And this we conceive to be no other than love, the love of God and of all mankind: the loving God with all our heart and soul and strength, as having first loved *us*, as the fountain of all the good we have received and of all we ever hope to enjoy; and the loving every soul which God hath made, every man on earth, as our own soul.

3. This love we believe to be the medicine of life, the never-failing remedy for all the evils of a disordered world, for all

the miseries and vices of men. Wherever this is, there are virtue and happiness, going hand in hand. There is humbleness of mind, gentleness, long-suffering, the whole image of God, and at the same time a "peace that passeth all understanding" and "joy unspeakable and full of glory":

> Eternal sunshine of the spotless mind;
> Each prayer accepted, and each wish resigned; . . .
> Desires composed, affections ever even,
> Tears that delight, and sighs that waft to heaven.

4. This religion we long to see established in the world, a religion of love and joy and peace, having its seat in the heart, in the inmost soul, but ever showing itself by its fruits, continually springing forth not only in all innocence—for "love works no ill to his neighbor"—but likewise in every kind of beneficence, in spreading virtue and happiness all around it.

5. This religion have we been following after for many years, as many know, if they would testify. But all this time, seeking wisdom we found it not; we were spending our strength in vain. And being now under full conviction of this, we declare it to all mankind. For we desire not that others should wander out of the way as we have done before them, but rather that they may profit by our loss, that they may go (though we did not, having then no man to guide us) the strait way to the religion of love, even by faith.

6. Now faith (supposing the Scripture to be of God) is πράγματων ἔλεγκος οὐ βλεπομένων, the demonstrative evidence of things unseen, the supernatural evidence of things invisible, not perceivable by eyes of flesh or by any of our natural senses or faculties. Faith is that divine evidence whereby the spiritual man discerns God and the things of God. It is with regard to the spiritual world what sense is with regard to the natural. It is the spiritual sensation of every soul that is born of God.

7. Perhaps you have not considered it in this view. I will then explain it a little further.

Faith, according to the scriptural account, is the eye of the newborn soul. Hereby every true believer in God "sees Him who is invisible." Hereby (in a more particular manner since life and immortality have been brought to light by the gospel) he sees "the light of the glory of God in the face of Jesus Christ" and "beholds what manner of love it is which the Father has bestowed upon us, that we" (who are born of the Spirit) "should be called the sons of God."

It is the ear of the soul, whereby a sinner "hears the voice of the Son of God and lives," even that voice which alone wakes the dead, "Son, your sins are forgiven you."

It is (if I may be allowed the expression) the palate of the soul. For hereby a believer "tastes the good word, and the powers of the world to come"; and hereby he both "tastes and sees that God is gracious," yes, and "merciful to him a sinner."

It is the feeling of the soul, whereby a believer perceives, through the "power of the Highest overshadowing him," both the existence and the presence of Him in whom we "live, move, and have our being," and indeed, the whole invisible world, the entire system of things eternal. And hereby, in particular, he feels "the love of God shed abroad in his heart."

8. "By this faith we are saved" from all uneasiness of mind, from the anguish of a wounded spirit, from discontent, from fear and sorrow of heart, from that inexpressible listlessness and weariness, both of the world and of ourselves, which we had so helplessly labored under for many years, especially when we were out of the hurry of the world and sunk into calm reflection. In this we find that love of God and of all mankind which we had elsewhere sought in vain. This we know and feel—and therefore cannot but declare—saves everyone that partakes of it both from sin and misery, from every unhappy and every unholy temper.

> Soft peace she brings, wherever she arrives;
> She builds our quiet as she forms our lives,
> Lays the rough paths of peevish nature even,
> And opens in each breast a little heaven.

9. If you ask, "Why then have not all men this faith, all, at least, who conceive it to be so happy a thing? Why do they not believe immediately?"—we answer (on the Scripture hypothesis), "It is the gift of God." No man is able to work it in himself. It is a work of omnipotence. It requires no less power thus to quicken a dead soul than to raise a body that lies in the grave. It is a new creation; and none can create a soul anew but He who at first created the heavens and the earth.

10. May not your own experience teach you this? Can *you* give yourself this faith? Is it now in your power to see, or hear, or taste, or feel God? Have you already, or can you raise in yourself, any perception of God or of an invisible world? I suppose you do not deny that there is an invisible world. You will not charge it in poor old Hesiod to Christian prejudice of education when he says, in those well known words,

> Millions of spiritual creatures walk the earth
> Unseen, whether we wake, or if we sleep.

Now is there any power in your soul whereby you discern either these or Him that created them? Or can all your wisdom and strength open an intercourse between yourself and the world of spirits? Is it in your power to burst the veil that is on your heart and let in the light of eternity? You know it is not. You not only do not but cannot (by your own strength) thus believe. The more you labor so to do, the more you will be convinced "it is the gift of God."

11. It is the *free gift* of God, which He bestows not on those who are worthy of His favor, not on such as . . . [were] previously holy and so *fit* to be crowned with all the blessings of His goodness, but on the ungodly and unholy, on those who till that hour were fit only for everlasting destruction, those in whom was no good thing and whose only plea was, "God, be merciful to me a sinner." No merit, no goodness in man, precedes the forgiving love of God. His pardoning mercy supposes nothing in us but a sense of mere sin and misery; and to all who see and feel and own their wants and their utter inability to remove them, God freely gives faith, for the sake of Him "in whom He is always well pleased."

12. This is a short rude sketch of the doctrine we teach. These are our fundamental principles; and we spend our lives in confirming others herein, and in a behavior suitable to them. . . .

46. Once more: can you or any man of reason think you were made for the life you now lead? You cannot possibly think so—at least, not till you tread the Bible under foot. The oracles of God bear you witness in every page (and your own heart agrees thereto) that you were made in the image of God, an incorruptible picture of the God of glory. And what are you even in your present state? An everlasting spirit, going to God. For what end then did He create you but to dwell with Him above this perishable world, to know Him, to love Him, to do His will, to enjoy Him for ever and ever! O look more deeply into yourself and into that Scripture which you profess to receive as the "Word of God," as "right concerning all things." There you will find a nobler, happier state described than it ever yet entered into your heart to conceive. But God has now revealed it to all those who "rejoice evermore" and "pray without ceasing" and "in everything give thanks" and "do His will on earth as it is done in heaven." For this you were made. Hereunto also you are called. O be not disobedient to the heavenly calling! At least, be not angry with those who would fain bring you to be a living witness of that religion "whose ways are" indeed "ways of pleasantness, and all her paths, peace."

47. Do you say in your heart: "I know all this already. I am not barely a man of reason. I am a religious man, for I not only avoid evil and do good but use all the means of grace. I am constantly at church, and at the Sacrament too. I say my prayers every day. I read many good books. I fast every thirtieth of January, and Good Friday." Do you indeed? Do you do all this? This you may do. You may go thus far and yet have no religion at all, no such religion as avails before God. Nay, much further than this, than you have ever gone yet, or so much as thought of going. For you may "give all your goods to feed the poor," yes, "your body to be burned," and yet very possibly, if St. Paul be a judge, have no charity, "no true religion."

48. This religion, which alone is of value before God, is the very thing you want. You want (and in wanting this, you want all) the religion of love. You do not love your neighbor as yourself, no more than you love God with all your heart. Ask your own heart now if it be not so? 'Tis plain you do not love God. If you did you would be happy in Him. But you know you are not happy. Your *formal* religion no more makes you happy than your neighbor's *gay* religion does him. O how much have you suffered for want of plain dealing! Can you now bear to hear the naked truth? You have the "form of godliness" but not "the power." You are a mere whited wall. Before the Lord your God I ask you, "Are you not?"

To [be] sure. For your "inward parts are very wickedness." You love "the creature more than the Creator." You are "a lover of pleasure more than a lover of God." A lover of God? You do not love God at all, no more than you love a stone. You cannot love God, for you love praise. You love the world; therefore the love of the Father is not in you.

49. You are on the brink of the pit, ready to be plunged into everlasting perdition. Indeed you "have a zeal for God, but not according to knowledge." O how terribly have you been deceived, posting to hell and fancying it was heaven! See at length that outward religion without inward is nothing—is far worse than nothing, being indeed no other than a solemn mockery of God. And *inward religion you have not.* You have not the "faith that works by love." Your faith (so called) is no living, saving principle. It is not the apostle's faith, "the substance (or subsistence) of things hoped for, the evidence of things not seen"—so far from it that this faith is the very thing which you call "enthusiasm." You are not content with being without it unless you blaspheme it too. You even revile that "life which is hid with Christ in God"—all seeing, tasting, hearing, feeling God. These things "are foolishness unto *you.*" No marvel, for "they are spiritually discerned."

50. O no longer shut your eyes against the light! Know you have a name that you live, but are dead. Your soul is utterly dead in sin, dead in pride, in vanity, in self-will, in sensuality, in love of the world. You are utterly dead to God. There is no intercourse between your soul and God. "You have neither seen Him" (by faith, as our Lord witnessed against them of old time) "nor heard His voice at any time." You have no spiritual "senses exercised to discern spiritual good and evil." You are angry at infidels, and are all the while as mere an infidel before God as they. You have "eyes that see not and ears that hear not." You have a *callous, unfeeling* heart.

51. Bear with me a little longer; my soul is distressed for you. "The god of this world has blinded your eyes" and you are "seeking death in the error of your life." Because you do not commit gross sin, because you give alms and go to the church and sacrament, you imagine that you are serving God; yet in very deed you are serving the Devil. For you are doing still your own will, not the will of God your Savior. You are pleasing yourself in all you do. Pride, vanity, and self-will (the genuine fruits of an earthly, sensual, devilish heart) pollute all your words and actions. You are in darkness, in the shadow of death. O that God would say to you in thunder, "Awake, you that sleep, and arise from the dead, and Christ shall give you light!" [Eph. 5:14].

52. But, blessed be God, He has not yet left Himself without witness!

> All are not lost! There be who faith prefer,
> Though few, and piety to God,

who know the power of faith and are no strangers to that inward vital religion, "the mind that was in Christ," "righteousness, and peace, and joy in the Holy Ghost." Of you who "have tasted the good word of God, and the powers of the world to come" would we be glad to learn if we have "erred from the faith" or walked contrary to "the truth as it is in Jesus." "Let the righteous smite me friendly, and reprove me," if haply that which is amiss may be done away and what is wanting supplied, 'till we all come "to the measure of the stature of the fulness of Christ."

53. Perhaps the first thing that now occurs to your mind relates to the doctrine which we teach. You have heard that we say, "Men may live without sin." And have you not heard that the Scripture says the same (we mean, without *committing* sin)? Does not St. Paul say plainly that those who believe do not "continue in sin," that they cannot "live any longer therein" (Rom. 6:1–2)? Does not St. Peter say, "He that has suffered in the flesh has ceased from sin, that he no longer should live to the desires of men, but to the will of God" (1 Peter 4:1–2)? And does not St. John say most expressly, "He that committeth sin is of the devil. . . . For this purpose the Son of God was manifested, that He might destroy the works of the devil. Whosoever is born of God does not commit sin, for His seed remains in him, and he cannot sin, because he is born of God" (1 John 3:8–9)? And again, "We know that whosoever is born of God sins not" (chap. 5:18)?

54. You see, then, it is not *we* that say this, but the Lord. These are not *our* words, but His. And who is he that replies against God? Who is able to make God a liar? Surely He will be "justified in His saying, and clear when He is judged"! Can you deny it? Have you not often felt a secret check when you were contradicting this great truth? And how often have you wished what you were taught to deny? Nay, can you help wishing for it at this moment? Do you not now earnestly desire to cease from sin, to commit it no more? Does not your soul pant after this glorious liberty of the sons of God? And what strong reason have you to expect it? Have you not had a foretaste of it already? Do you not remember the time when God first lifted up the light of His countenance upon you? Can it ever be forgotten, the day when the "candle of the Lord" first "shone upon your head"?

> Butter and honey did you eat,
> And, lifted up on high,
> You saw the clouds beneath your feet,
> And rode upon the sky.
>
> Far, far above all earthly things,
> Triumphantly you rode;
> You soared to heaven on eagles' wings,
> And found, and talked with God.

You then had power not to commit sin. You found the apostle's words strictly true: "He that is begotten of God keeps himself, and that wicked one touches him not." But those whom you took to be experienced Christians telling you this was only the time of your espousals, this could not last always, you must come down from the mount, and the like, shook your faith. You looked at men more than God, and so became weak and like another man. Whereas had you then had any to guide you according to the truth of God, had you then heard the doctrine which now you blame, you . . . |would have| never fallen from your steadfastness but . . . |would have| found that in this sense also "the gifts and calling of God are without repentance."

55. Have you not another objection nearly allied to this, namely that we preach perfection? True, but what perfection? The term you cannot object to, because it is scriptural. All the difficulty is to fix the meaning of it according to the Word of God. And this we have done again and again, declaring to all the world that Christian perfection does not imply an exemption from ignorance or mistake or infirmities or temptations, but that it does imply the being so "crucified with Christ" as to be able to testify, "I live not, but Christ lives in me" (Gal. 2:20) and has "purified my heart by faith" (Acts 15:9). It does imply the "casting down every high thing that exalts itself against the knowledge of God, and bringing into captivity every thought to the obedience of Christ." It does imply the "being holy as He that has called us is holy, in all manner of conversation" (2 Cor. 10:5, 1 Peter 1:15) and, in a word, the "loving the Lord our God with all our heart, and serving him with all our strength."

56. Now is it possible for any who believes the Scripture to deny one tittle of this? You cannot. You dare not. You would not for the world. You know it is the pure word of God. And this is the whole of what we preach. This is the height and depth of what we (with St. Paul) call perfection—a state of soul devoutly to be wished for by all who have tasted of the love of God. O pray for it without ceasing. It is the one thing you want. "Come with boldness to the throne of grace" and be assured that when you ask this of God you shall "have the petition you ask of Him." We know indeed that "to man"—to the natural man—"this is impossible." But we know also that as "no work is impossible with God," so "all things are possible to him that believes."

57. For we are saved by faith. But have you not heard this urged as another objection against us, that we preach salvation by faith alone? And does not St. Paul do the same thing? "By grace," says he, "You are saved through faith." Can any words be more express? And elsewhere, "Believe in the Lord Jesus and you shall be saved" (Acts 16:34).

What we mean by this (if it has not been sufficiently explained already) is that we are saved from our sins only by a confidence in the love of God. As soon as we "behold what manner of love it is which the Father has bestowed upon us," "we love Him (as the apostle observes) because He first loved us." And then is that commandment written in our heart, "that he who loves God love his brother also"; from which love of God and man, meekness, humbleness of mind, and all holy tempers spring. Now these are the very essence of salvation, of Christian salvation, salvation from sin. And from these outward salvation flows, that is, holiness of life and conversation. Well, and are not these things so? If you know in whom you have believed you need no further witnesses.

58. But perhaps you doubt whether that faith whereby we are thus saved implies such a trust and confidence in God as we describe. You cannot think faith implies assurance, an assurance of the love of God to our souls, of His being now reconciled to us, and having forgiven all our sins. And this we freely confess, that if number of voices is to decide the question we must give it up at once, for you have on your side not only some who desire to be Christians indeed but all nominal Christians in every place, and the Romish Church, one and all. Nay, these last are so vehement in your defense that in the famed Council of Trent they have decreed: "If any man hold *fiduciam* (trust, confidence, or assurance of pardon) to be essential to faith, let him be accursed."

59. If we consider the time when this decree was passed, namely, just after the publication of our |Anglican| homilies, it will appear more than probable that the very design of the Council was to anathematize the Church of England as being now convict, by her own Confession of Faith, of "that damnable and heretical doctrine."* For the very words in the Homily on Salvation** are:

> Even the devils ... believe that Christ was born of a virgin; ... that He wrought all kind of miracles, declaring Himself very God; ... that for our sakes He suffered a most painful death, to redeem us from death everlasting.... These articles of our faith the devils believe, and so they believe all that is written in the Old and New Testament.... And yet for all this faith they be but devils. They remain still in their damnable estate, lacking the very true Christian faith.
>
> The right and true Christian faith is, not only to believe the Holy Scriptures and the articles of our faith are true, but also to have a sure *trust* and *confidence* ... to be saved from everlasting damnation through Christ.

Or, as it is expressed a little after, "a sure trust and confidence which a man has in God, that by the merits of Christ his sins are forgiven and he reconciled to the favor of God."

---

*Gerald R. Cragg, ed., T*he Works of John Wesley*, vol. 11 (New York: Oxford University, 1975), p. 68n., explains Wesley's error in chronology that prompted him in later editions to abridge severely this sentence.

**In the Church of England's *Book of Common Prayer*.

60. Indeed the Bishop of Rome says, "If any man hold this, let him be *anathema maranatha*." But 'tis to be hoped papal anathemas do not move *you*. You are a member of the Church of England. Are you? Then the controversy is at an end. Then hear the Church: faith is "a sure trust which a man has in God, that his sins are forgiven." Or if you are not, whether you hear our church or no, at least hear the Scriptures. Hear believing Job declaring his faith: "I know that my Redeemer lives." Hear Thomas (when having seen, he believed) crying out, "My Lord and my God." Hear St. Paul clearly describing the nature of *his* faith: "The life I now live I live by faith in the Son of God, who loved *me* and gave himself for *me*." Hear (to mention no more) all the believers who were with Paul when he wrote to the Colossians, bearing witness: "We give thanks unto the Father, . . . who *has delivered* us from the power of darkness, and *has translated* us into the kingdom of His dear Son, in whom we have redemption through His blood, even *the forgiveness of sins*" (Col. 5:12, 13, 14).

61. But what need have we of distant witnesses? You have a witness in your own breast. For am I not speaking to one that loves God? How came *you* then to love Him at first? Was it not because you knew that He loved you? Did you, could you love God at all, 'til you "tasted and saw that He was gracious," that He was merciful to you a sinner? What avails then controversy or strife of words? "Out of your own mouth"! You own you had no love of God till you were sensible of His love to you. And whatever expressions any sinner who loves God uses to denote God's love to him, you will always, upon examination, find that they directly or indirectly imply forgiveness. Pardoning love is still at the root of all. He who was offended is now reconciled. The new song which God puts in every mouth is always to that effect: "O Lord, I will praise You. Though You were angry with me, Your anger is turned away. . . . Behold, God is my salvation. I will trust and not be afraid, for the Lord Jehovah is my strength and my song; he is also become my salvation" (Isa. 12:1, 2).

62. A confidence, then, in a pardoning God is essential to a true faith. The forgiveness of sins is one of the first of those unseen things whereof faith is the evidence. And if you are sensible of this, will you quarrel with us concerning an indifferent circumstance of it? Will you think it an important objection that we assert that this faith is usually given *in a moment?* First let me entreat you to read over that authentic account of God's dealings with men, the Acts of the Apostles. In this treatise you will find how He wrought from the beginning on those who received remission of sins by faith. And can you find one of these (except perhaps St. Paul) who did not receive it in a moment? But abundance you find of those who did, besides Cornelius and the three thousand. And to this also agrees the experience of those who now receive the heavenly gift. Three or four exceptions only have I found in the course of several years. (Perhaps you yourself may be added to that number, and one or two more whom you have known.) But all the rest of those who from time to time among us have believed in the Lord Jesus were in a moment brought "from darkness to light, and from the power of Satan unto God."

THE FIRST ANNUAL
METHODIST CONFERENCE

Monday, June 25, 1744

INTRODUCTION

By the summer of Wesley's fifth year of preaching the vision of Christian perfection he had come to in the fall of 1739, the Methodist movement had grown large enough for its founder to summon four of the Anglican clergy who were in fellowship with him to a consultation with him and his brother Charles on the course of the movement. They agreed to meet regularly and to invite such lay preachers as they wished. Four of the most prominent ones then in London were brought into that first "conference." After some preliminary conversations, as the minutes tell us, they took up a series of twenty-six questions having to do with justification and regeneration. Those questions, and what was undoubtedly Wesley's answer to them, given after he had received the comments of all who wished to speak, are recorded below. The copy used here, now the standard one, is from John Bennet's version of the minutes, which Wesley relied upon. They appeared in 1894 as the first *Publication* of the Wesley Historical Society.

The next morning the group took up the doctrine of sanctification, in both its progressive and instantaneous aspects. Clearly, the order of salvation, as it is called, has remained constant in Wesleyanism from the early years of that decade to the present. But just as clearly, the task of helping both preachers and lay persons to understand these doctrines has also been constant.

Throughout these minutes we see that when dealing with his own people Wesley's authority was Scripture. He handled it as rationally as he was able and in the light of the experience of saving faith. He did not refer here to tradition, ancient or modern, though in composing such theological essays as his *Earnest Appeal to Men of Reason and Religion* and

Farther Appeal Wesley drew heavily upon the writings of the early church fathers and the Anglican divines of the previous two centuries. But for Methodists, the Bible and their own experience of the grace of God seemed to be enough.

❖   ❖   ❖

The following persons being met at the foundry, John Wesley, Charles Wesley, John Hodges, Henry Piers, Samuel Taylor, and John Meriton, after some time spent in prayer, the design of our meeting was proposed, namely, to consider,

1. What to teach;
2. How to teach; and
3. What to do, that is, how to regulate our doctrine, discipline, and practice.

But first it was inquired whether any of our lay brethren should be present at this conference, and it was agreed to invite from time to time such of them as we should think proper. 'Twas then asked, "Which of them shall we invite today?" The answer was, "Thomas Richards, Thomas Maxfield, John Bennet, and John Downes," who were accordingly brought in. Then was read as follows:

> It is desired that all things may be considered as in the immediate presence of God, that we may meet with a single eye and as little children who have everything to learn, that every point may be examined from the foundation, that every person may speak freely whatever is in his heart, and that every question proposed may be fully debated and bolted to the bran.

The first preliminary question was then proposed, namely, how far does each of us agree to submit to the unanimous judgment of the rest? It was answered: in speculative things each can only submit so far as his judgment shall be convinced; in every practical point, so far as we can without wounding our consciences. To the second preliminary question, namely, how far should any of us mention to others what may be mentioned here, it was replied: "Not one word which may be here spoken of persons should be mentioned elsewhere; nothing at all, unless so far as we may be convinced the glory of God requires it. And from time to time we will consider on each head, is it for the glory of God that what we have now spoken should be mentioned again?"

About seven o'clock we began to consider the doctrine of justification, the questions relating to which were as follows, with the substance of the answers thereto:

Q. 1. What is it to be justified?

A. To be pardoned and received into God's favor and into such a state that, if we continue therein, we shall be finally saved.

Q. 2. Is faith the condition of justification?

A. Yes, for everyone who believes not is condemned and everyone who believes is justified.

Q. 3. But must not repentance and works meet for repentance go before faith?

A. Without doubt, if by repentance you mean conviction of sin, and by works meet for repentance, obeying God as far as we can, forgiving our brother, leaving off from evil, doing good, and using His ordinances according to the power we have received.

Q. 4. What is faith?

A. Faith, in general, is a divine, supernatural $\varepsilon\lambda\varepsilon\gamma\kappa o\varsigma$ ["evidence," "manifestation"] of things not seen, that is, of past, future, or spiritual things; 'tis a spiritual sight of God and the things of God. Therefore repentance is a low species of faith, that is, a supernatural sense of an offended God. Justifying faith is a supernatural inward sense or sight of God in Christ reconciling the world unto Himself. First, a sinner is convinced by the Holy Ghost, "Christ loved me and gave Himself for me." This is that faith by which he is justified, or pardoned, the moment he receives it. Immediately the same Spirit bears witness, "You are pardoned, you have redemption in His blood." And this is saving faith, whereby the love of God is shed abroad in his heart.

Q. 5. Have all true Christians this faith? May not a man be justified and not know it?

A. That all true Christians have this faith, even such a faith as implies an assurance of God's love, appears from Romans 8:15, Ephesians 4:32, 2 Corinthians 13:5, Hebrews 8:10, 1 John 4:10, and, last, 1 John 5:19. And that no man can be justified and not know it appears further from the very nature of things, for faith after repentance is ease after pain, rest after toil, light after darkness, and from the immediate as well as distant fruits.

Q. 6. But may not a man go to heaven without it?

A. It does not appear from Holy Writ that a man who hears the gospel can (Mark 16:16), whatever a heathen may do (Rom. 2:14).

Q. 7. What are the immediate fruits of justifying faith?

A. Peace, joy, love, power over all outward sin, and power to keep down all inward sin.

Q. 8. Does any one believe who has not the witness in himself, or any longer than he sees, loves, and obeys God?

A. We apprehend not, "seeing God" being the very essence of faith, [and] love and obedience the inseparable properties of it.

Q. 9. What sins are consistent with justifying faith?

A. No wilful sin. If a believer wilfully sins, he thereby forfeits his pardon. Neither is it possible he should have justifying faith again without previously repenting.

Q. 10. Must every believer come into a state of doubt or fear or darkness? Will he do so unless by ignorance or unfaithfulness? Does God otherwise withdraw Himself?

A. It is certain a believer need never again come into condemnation. It seems he need not come into a state of doubt or fear or darkness and that (ordinarily at least) he will not, unless by ignorance and unfaithfulness. Yet it is true that the first joy does seldom last long, that it is commonly followed by doubts and fears, and that God usually permits very great heaviness before any large manifestation of Himself.

Q. 11. Are works necessary to the continuance of faith?

A. Without doubt, for a man may forfeit the gift of God either by sins of omission or commission.

Q. 12. Can faith be lost but for want of works?

A. It cannot but through disobedience.

Q. 13. How is faith made perfect by works?

A. The more we exert our faith, the more 'tis increased. To him that has, more and more is given.

Q. 14. St. Paul says, Abraham was not justified by works; St. James, he was justified by works. Do not they then contradict each other?

A. No. (1) Because they do not speak of the same justification. St. Paul speaks of that justification which was when Abraham was 75 years old, above 20 years before Isaac was born, St. James of that justification which was when he offered up Isaac on the altar. (2) Because they do not speak of the same works. St. Paul speaks of works that precede faith, St. James of works that spring from faith.

Q. 15. In what sense is Adam's sin imputed to all mankind?

A. In Adam all die, that is, (1) our bodies then became mortal. |and| (2) our souls died, that is, were disunited from God. (3) And hence we are all born with a sinful, devilish nature by reason whereof, (4) we all are children of wrath, liable to death eternal. Romans 5:18; Ephesians 2:3.

Q. 16. In what sense is the righteousness of Christ imputed to believers, or to all mankind?

A. We do not find it affirmed expressly in Scripture that God imputes the righteousness of Christ to any, although we do find that faith is imputed unto us for righteousness. That text, "As by one man's disobedience all men were made sinners, so by the obedience of one all were made righteous," we conceive means, by the merits of Christ all men are cleared from the guilt of Adam's actual sin. We conceive further that through the obedience and death of Christ, (1) the bodies of all men become immortal after the Resurrection; (2) their souls recover a capacity of spiritual life and (3) an actual seed or spark thereof; (4) all believers become children of grace, (5) are reunited to God, and (6) made partakers of the divine nature.

Q. 17. Have we not then unawares leaned too much towards Calvinism?

A. It seems we have.

Q. 18. Have we not also leaned towards antinomianism?

A. We are afraid we have.

Q. 19. What is antinomianism?

A. The doctrine which makes void the law through faith.

Q. 20. What are the main pillars thereof?

A. (1) That Christ abolished the moral law; (2) that Christians therefore are not obliged to observe it; (3) that one branch of Christian liberty is liberty from obeying the commandments of God; (4) that it is bondage to do a thing because it is commanded or forbear it because it is forbidden; (5) that a believer is not obliged to use the ordinances of God or to do good works; |and| (6) that a preacher ought not to exhort to good works—not unbelievers because it is hurtful, not believers because it is needless.

Q. 21. What was the occasion of St. Paul writing his Epistle to the Galatians?

A. The coming of certain men among the Christians who taught, "Except you be circumcised, and keep the whole law of Moses, you cannot be saved."

Q. 22. What is his main design therein?

A. To prove, (1) that no man can be justified or saved by the works of the law, either moral or ritual; |and| (2) that every believer is justified by faith in Christ, without the works of the law.

Q. 23. What does he mean by the works of the law?

A. All works that do not spring from faith in Christ.

Q. 24. What is meant by being under the law?

A. Under the Mosaic dispensation.

Q. 25. What law has Christ abolished?

A. The ritual law of Moses.

Q. 26. What is meant by liberty?

A. Liberty (1) from the law |and| (2) from sin.

OF PREACHING CHRIST

A personal letter from John Wesley

INTRODUCTION

I close these selections with a personal letter about progressive sanctification, not from Whitefield, whose proclamation of that idea is well known, but from John Wesley, in response to criticisms from an evangelical layman. Wesley noted in a surviving fragment of his diary for the day of his response, December 20, 1751, that he trusted it would "cut up the controversy" over the subject "by the roots." Wesley probably circulated the manuscript among his closest followers, and finally published it in *The Arminian Magazine* for June, 1779. The copy provided here is from that printed version. Francis Asbury republished it in the Philadelphia *Arminian Magazine* in October, 1789.

The letter defines what Wesley believes is "preaching the law" and "preaching the gospel." The former is "explaining and enforcing the commands of Christ . . . in the Sermon on the Mount." To Charles G. Finney, an evangelist of a later day, and to all too many American evangelists who have followed in his train, the law applicable since Christ rests much more on the commands and threats of awesome punishment found in the Old Testament, than upon Christ's searching sermon about inward holiness in the New. "Preaching the gospel," Wesley states, is presenting persons convinced of their sin and lostness with the scriptural promises of salvation, in such a way that the Holy Spirit can create in them saving faith.

Wesley, as always, was concerned about those "gospel preachers" who neglected moral discipline and allowed those who had been born again to drift backward to lives of unworthiness. The law, he said—that is, the Sermon on the Mount—is for Christians "a branch of the glorious liberty of the sons of God." It gives them freedom from bondage to sin, by continually revealing to them the love of Christ.

This kind of preaching is far removed from the legalism that has always beset evangelical preaching. For this, Wesley said, would both nourish and strengthen the soul and comfort it with the assurance that growth in sanctity flows from feasting on the Word of the Lord. As Wesley put it, law and gospel, thus understood, must be preached "both at once, or both in one." For law, in the deepest sense, is gospel; and gospel is the promise of grace to keep the law.

Both Wesley and George Whitefield made such preaching the passion of their lives. Its rebirth is giving a new sense of moral purpose to the modern evangelical awakening.

❖   ❖   ❖

London, December 20, 1751.

My dear friend,

The point you speak of in your letter of September 21 is of a very important nature. I have had many serious thoughts concerning it, particularly for some months last past. Therefore, I was not willing to speak hastily or slightly of it, but rather delayed till I could consider it thoroughly.

I mean by "preaching the gospel," preaching the love of God to sinners, preaching the life, death, resurrection, and intercession of Christ, with all the blessings which in consequence thereof are freely given to true believers.

By "preaching the law" I mean explaining and enforcing the commands of Christ briefly comprised in the Sermon on the Mount.

Now it is certain, preaching the gospel to penitent sinners "begets faith," that it "sustains and increases spiritual life in true believers."

Nay, sometimes it "teaches and guides" them that believe; yes, and "convinces them that believe not."

So far all are agreed. But what is the stated means of "feeding and comforting" believers? What is the means, as of "begetting spiritual life" where it is not, so of "sustaining and increasing" it where it is?

Here they divide. Some think, preaching the law only; others, preaching the gospel only. I think, neither the one nor the other, but duly mixing both, in every place if not in every sermon.

I think the right method of preaching is this. At our first beginning to preach at any place—after a general declaration of the love of God to sinners and His willingness that they should be saved—to preach the law in the strongest, the closest, the most searching manner possible, only intermixing the gospel here and there and showing it, as it were, afar off.

After more and more persons are convinced of sin, we may mix more and more of the gospel in order to "beget faith," to raise into spiritual life those whom the law has slain; but this is not to be done too hastily either. Therefore it is not expedient wholly to omit the law, not only because we may well suppose that many of our hearers are still unconvinced but because otherwise there is danger that many who are convinced will heal their own wounds slightly. Therefore it is only in private converse with a thoroughly convinced sinner that we should preach nothing but the gospel.

If, indeed, we could suppose a whole congregation to be thus convinced, we should need to preach only the gospel. And the same we might do if our whole congregation were supposed to be newly justified. But when these grow in grace and in the knowledge of Christ, a wise builder would preach the law to them again, only taking particular care to place every part of it in a gospel light as not only a command but a privilege also, as a branch of the glorious liberty of the sons of God. He would take equal care to remind them that this is not the cause but the fruit of their acceptance with God; that other cause, "other foundation, can no man lay than that which is laid, even Jesus Christ"; that we are still forgiven and accepted only for the sake of what He has done and suffered for us; and that all true obedience springs from love to Him, grounded on His first loving us. He would labor, therefore, in preaching any part of the law, to keep the love of Christ continually before their eyes, that thence they might draw fresh life, vigor, and strength to run the way of His commandments.

Thus would he preach the law even to those who are pressing on to the mark. But to those who are careless or drawing back he would preach it in another manner, nearly as he did before they were convinced of sin. To those meanwhile who are earnest but feebleminded, he would preach the gospel chiefly, yet variously intermixing more or less of the law according to their various necessities.

By preaching the law in the manner above described, he would teach them how to walk in Him whom they had received. Yes, and the same means (the main point wherein it seems your mistake lies) would both "sustain and increase" their "spiritual life." For the commands are food as well as promises—food equally wholesome, equally substantial. These also, duly applied, not only direct but likewise "nourish and strengthen" the soul.

Of this you appear not to have the least conception; therefore I will endeavor to explain it. I ask then, "Do not all the children of God experience that when God gives them to see deeper into His blessed law, whenever He gives a new degree of light, He gives likewise a new degree of strength?" Now I see, He that loves me bids me do this. And now I feel I can do it through Christ strengthening me.

Thus light and strength are given by the same means and frequently in the same moment, although sometimes there is a space between. For instance, I hear the command, "Let your communication be always in grace, meet to minister grace to the hearers." God gives me more light into this command. I see the exceeding height and depth of it. At the same time I see (by the same light from above) how far I have fallen short. I am ashamed; I am humbled before God. I earnestly desire to keep it better; I pray to Him that has loved me for more strength, and I have the petition I ask of Him. Thus the law not only convicts the unbeliever and enlightens the believing soul, but also conveys food to a believer, sustains and increases his spiritual life and strength.

And if it increases his spiritual life and strength, it cannot but increase his comfort also. For doubtless the more we are alive to God, the more we shall rejoice in Him; the greater measure of His strength we receive, the greater will be our consolation also.

And all this, I conceive, is clearly declared in one single passage of Scripture: "The law of the Lord is perfect, *converting the soul*; the testimony of the Lord is sure, *making wise* the simple. The statutes of the Lord are right, *rejoicing the heart*; the commandment of the Lord is pure, *enlightening the eyes*. *More to be desired* are they than gold, yes, than much fine gold; *sweeter* also than honey and the honeycomb." They are both food and medicine; they both refresh, strengthen, and nourish the soul.

Not that I would advise to preach the law without the gospel any more than the gospel without the law. Undoubtedly both should be preached in their turns; yes, both at once, or both in one. All the conditional promises are instances of this. They are law and gospel mixed together.

According to this model, I should advise every preacher continually to preach the law—the law grafted upon, tempered by, and animated with the spirit of the gospel. I advise him to declare, explain, and enforce every command of God. But meantime to declare in every sermon (and the more explicitly the better) that the first and great command to a Christian is, "Believe in the Lord Jesus Christ"; that Christ is all in all, our "wisdom, righteousness, sanctification, and redemption"; that all life, love, and strength are from Him alone, and all freely given to us through faith. And it will ever be found that the law thus preached both enlightens and strengthens the soul, that it both nourishes and teaches, that it is the guide, "food, medicine, and stay" of the believing soul.

Thus all the apostles built up believers—witness all the epistles of Sts. Paul, James, Peter, and John. And upon this plan all the Methodists first set out. In this manner, not only my brother and I, but Mr. [Thomas] Maxfield, [John] Nelson, James Jones, [Thomas] Westell, and [Jonathan] Reeves all preached at the beginning.

By this preaching it pleased God to work those mighty effects in London, Bristol, Kingswood, Yorkshire, and Newcastle. By means of this, twenty-nine persons received remission of sins in one day at Bristol only, most of them while I was opening and enforcing in this manner our Lord's Sermon upon the Mount. . . .

Index